1000727030

	DATE DUE	
RECEIVED 2 7 199 NOV 0 1 1996	0 8 MAR 2002	
APR 2 5 1997	1 0 APR 2002	
NOV 0 6 1997		
APR 0 3 1998		
1 8 OCT 1998		
FEB 1 4 2000		
1 8 OCT 2000		
2 5 OCT 2001		

Adolescent Suicidal Behavior
A Family Systems Model

Research in Clinical Psychology, No. 7

Peter E. Nathan, Series Editor

Professor and Chairman
Department of Clinical Psychology
Rutgers, the State University

Other Titles in This Series

Adolescent Suicidal Behavior
A Family Systems Model

by
Roma J. Heillig

UMI RESEARCH PRESS
Ann Arbor, Michigan

Produced and distributed by
UMI Research Press
an imprint of
University Microfilms International
Ann Arbor, Michigan 48106

Library of Congress Cataloging in Publication Data

Heillig, Roma J. (Roma Jocene)
Adolescent suicidal behavior.

(Research in clinical psychology ; no. 7)
Revision of thesis (Ph.D.)–University of Massachusetts,
1980.
Bibliography: p.
Includes index.
1. Youth–Suicidal behavior. 2. Youth–Family relationships. 3. Deprivation (Psychology) 4. Separation (Psychology) I. Title. II. Series. [DNLM: 1. Adolescent
behavior. 2. Family. 3. Suicide. W1 RE227FD no.7 /
HV 6546 H466a]

HV6546.H44 1983   616.85'8445071'088055   83-3594
ISBN 0-8357-1390-3

A drop which fell from a rain-cloud
Was disturbed by the extent of the sea:
'Who am I in the ocean's vastness?
If IT *is,* then I am *not:*'
While it saw itself with the eye of contempt
A shell nurtured it in its bosom.
The heavens so fostered things
That it became a celebrated, a royal Pearl:
Becoming high from being low
It knocked on the door of nothingness:
Until Being came about.

-Saadi, 13th Century

Contents

List of Figures and Tables

List of Figures

List of Tables

Acknowledgments

I would like to express my gratitude to those who helped me on the original project. Harold Jarmon, Bea Chorover, Alvin Winder, the late Cynthia Wild Cowgill, and my husband, Jess Morris were most generous with their conceptual contributions and emotional support.

I would like to acknowledge and thank the mental health facilities that offered me their utmost cooperation in the task of locating appropriate participants for the research presented in this text.

Finally, I would like to express my respect for the participants themselves who had the courage to share intimate and often painful details of their lives with me.

1

Introduction

Historically, the phenomenon of suicide has been understood and accounted for along a broad spectrum of paradigms ranging from the primitive explanations of early man to the more complex and theoretically sophisticated models proposed by contemporary science. Self-destruction has been considered a moral-religious problem, a philosophical dilemma, an organic disease entity, and most recently a psycho-social event. This latter and most recent paradigm shift occurred at the beginning of the twentieth century when what had been up until then contrasting theoretical and empirical approaches to suicide began to converge toward a specific contextual point. At that time, theorists began to view self-destruction within a framework which emphasized the importance of human behavior and, specifically, the role of the individual and society at large in the etiology of self-destruction. In short, suicide became an entity within the newly created paradigm of social science.

Two theorists, Emile Durkheim and Sigmund Freud, were primarily responsible for the introduction of suicide into the social sciences. Freud (1957) emphasized the etiological significance of phenomena internal to the individual such as biological drives and psychodynamic motivation with regard to self-destruction. Durkheim (1951), taking an anti-reductionist position, concentrated on factors external to the individual, primarily stressing society, its structure, its events, and its "collective" influence in the development of suicidal behavior and ideation. Although their foci differed, these two theorists generated a broad social science paradigm within which both psychological and sociological theories of suicide began to develop.

As is evident from the copious and at times contradictory literature on suicide, this paradigm has not yet dictated a uniform conceptual approach to suicide, but rather has generated a series of approaches which attempt to examine and explain self-destruction from a number of etiological perspectives. Specifically, within the discipline of psychology, these approaches fall along what may be regarded as a psycho-social continuum with formulations which emphasize purely intrapersonal factors in the etiology of suicide on one end (Zilboorg, 1936; Menninger, 1938; and Beck, 1967) and conceptualizations which stress an interactional-systems approach on the other (Speck, 1968 and Richman, 1971). Interpersonal or more strictly dyadic theories of suicide fall between the two (Stengel, 1958 and Kobler & Stotland, 1964). The theories represented along particular sections of this continuum to some extent embody the process of cross-fertilization which occurred between the psychological and sociological fields after Durkheim and Freud. However, these attempts at integrating the two perspectives have largely proved unsatisfactory because they have failed to do justice to the complementary relationship between the individual and his social context in the determination of suicidal ideation and behavior.

One factor which has impeded the development of an integrative etiological view of self-destruction involves the choice of empirical context. In order to capture the interplay between the individual and his social environment, does one study the individual, the social environment or both; and if both, which unit of the social environment is to be selected for investigation. A review of the theoretical and empirical work on suicide reveals that there has been a cross-theoretical consensus about an important social unit of focus with regard to self-destruction. The unit which has emerged as a common denominator for almost all conceptual approaches to suicide is the family. Focus on this social unit can be traced to the very earliest conceptions of suicide within the social sciences. While their theoretical approaches differed, both Durkheim and Freud endorsed the importance of the family in relation to self-destruction. Although it is more apparent in his philosophical than his psychological writings, Freud strongly felt that society, group institutions, and the family played a role in the determination of individual behavior. Specifically, Freud's notion of the "superego," a part of man's psyche shaped by the moral demands of society, looks remarkably similar to Durkheim's idea of the "collective conscience," a regulating body which largely guides and determines the actions of individuals within a society and maintains social cohesiveness. Thus, each man stressed, in varying degrees, the importance of the moral demands of society in the determination of human behavior. More importantly, each theorist recognized the family as a crucial unit through which moral demands are made explicit. Durkheim pointed to the necessity of a cohesive family structure and the enactment of certain family roles in order that these moral demands be communicated effectively to the individual. Freud stressed the importance and presence of family members, particularly parents, in the formation of a healthy superego. Both theorists regarded the healthy family as playing an important preventative role with regard to self-destruction. For Durkheim, the family prevented the individual from becoming susceptible to the society's collective inclination toward suicide. For Freud, the family provided an atmosphere where the individual could develop a superego capable of helping him resist instinctual self-destructive impulses.

Theories generated by the basic models of Durkheim and Freud also acknowledge the role of the family unit in the determination of suicide. Intrapersonal perspectives spotlight the family in their emphasis on the developmental processes of the individual; interpersonal approaches consider disruption in family life as a prime determinant of self-destructive behavior; and interactional-systems theories have chosen the family as a main target of investigation stressing the importance of family interchange. It is noteworthy that 50 percent, if not more, of the empirical work on suicide involves investigation of the topic in relation to some aspect of family life. In addition, upon closer examination, it becomes clear that the progression of theories and empirical investigation since Durkheim and Freud has served to sharpen and refine the nature of the original link between the family and suicide proposed by the two theorists. To date, this process has reached its highest point within the interactive-systems model of suicide which aims at delineating the relationship between the family and self-destruction.

The interactional-systems model which focuses on the role of interactive patterns and processes in relation to suicidal behavior is a relatively new and unexplored one. Generally, this model assumes that the problems of pathology of a social group or system are often expressed through one of the individuals who is a part of that system. Thus, psychopathology is regarded as a manifestation of a group problem rather than as an expression of individual difficulty. Within this framework, suicide, in particular, "is regarded as a symptom of family system malfunction, expressed via one member of the system" (Speck, 1968). At present, a significant body of research has not yet been conducted on the problem of suicide and the family system. Currently, there exists a small body of anecdotal data, a few investigations which attempt to isolate one or two patterns of interaction or communication relevant to families with a suicidal member, and only one systematic comprehensive investigation which attempts to identify and discuss multiple characteristics of a family system with a suicidal member.

Speck (1968) presents two case studies of families with a suicidal member. Although his work seems primarily to be a vehicle through which to communicate his general ideas about family therapy, he does introduce the notion that suicidal symptoms in a family member often function to secure a family goal or to meet family needs. For example, in his initial case presentation and discussion he notes that the suicidal family member, by attempting suicide and subsequently convalescing in the home, helps justify a basic and seemingly necessary family pattern. That is, the family uses the symptoms as an excuse to stay within the home and to maintain their isolation from the outside world.

Chazan (1972) offers a more empirically focused discussion in that she uses her case materials to illustrate a particular thesis. Deriving the motive of hostility from Freudian theory and the supposition that suicide has communicative impact from the work of Stengel (1958), she reverses the two notions and hypothesizes that suicide in a family member is a response to unspoken or implicit death wishes from other family members. Suicide occurs when hostility is communicated by others to the victim. There is a body of empirical evidence which lends support to this notion. Several investigations (Rosenbaum, 1970; Rosenberg & Latimer, 1966; Meerloo, 1959; and Sabbath, 1971) have demonstrated that individuals, particularly children who attempt suicide, are involved in relationships in which they are the recipients of hostile and aggressive communication from significant others.

Generally speaking, the interactive-systems model considers communication as an important and revealing aspect of a family's level of functioning. A number of empiricists have made an effort to investigate the nature of the communication in families with a suicidal member. Schrut (1964), studying individuals seeking help at the Los Angeles Suicide Prevention Center, found that a majority of his sample reported a history of having a negative self-concept, as experiencing a particular proneness to guilt feelings, and as engaging in self-destructive acts. Schrut reports that these reactions were in response to a family situation in which the parents had sensitized their children to guilt feelings indirectly conveying to the children over a long period of time that they were a "burden." Schrut like Chazan adheres to the notion that unspoken and implicit negative communications exist within a family system and that such communications may have a potentially destructive effect.

Other studies have examined the lack of effectiveness of communication in families with a suicidal member. Yusin (1972) found that parents were unable to empathize with their child's emotional or suicidal crisis and subsequently, through withdrawal or silence, communicate a lack of concern or an indifferent attitude. As a result, the suicidal person is the recipient of a rejecting message with the implicit content that those around him don't care whether he lives or dies. An investigation of suicidal adolescents and their families, conducted by Teicher and Jacobs (1966), illustrated that, in general, parents in their sample were unaware of at least one-third of their children's problems and that, in addition, the parents attributed to the adolescents problems which did not exist. Finally, Tuckman and Connon (1962) found that one-third of their sample of parents of suicidal adolescents were totally ignorant as to the circumstances surrounding or leading up to the suicidal act of their children. These investigations suggest that, in families with a suicidal member, there may exist interactive disturbances which result in negative and hostile messages preempting empathetic and positive communication.

A comprehensive and systematic study of families with a suicidal member by Richman (1971) lends support to a number of the previously discussed findings and also isolates several additional characteristics of such families. Studying 100 families with suicidal members, Richman identified 14 patterns of family functioning which appeared characteristic of a majority of his sample. He hypothesizes that all of these patterns combine to form a unique pattern of family functioning which he calls the "suicidal family system." The following is a list and brief explanation of each of the 14 characteristics.

1. *Intolerance for separation*: A majority of suicidal families experience more incidents of loss or separation than non-suicidal families. As a result, separation is an overly sensitive issue and a situation in which separation is

involved often precipitates a suicidal crisis in one of the family members. These families appear to live literally by the motto, "'til death do us part."

2. *Symbiosis without empathy*: Suicidal families maintain symbiotic relationships in which the suicidal individual is exploited by other family members. The needs of the suicidal member are not acknowledged or recognized as other family members are not able to see the suicidal person as separate from themselves. When the needs of the suicidal individual go unheeded, he receives the communication not to be.

3. *Fixation upon infantile patterns*: Suicidal families are threatened by the ideas of growth, maturity, and change since these notions are often equated with loss and separation. Thus, the family encourages fixation on early infantile patterns to prevent growth and subsequent searation.

4. *Fixation upon earlier social roles*: A pattern of role disturbance and role failure is ever present in the areas of social and personal functioning in suicidal families. Suicidal family members, particularly parents, are often playing out social roles which characterized an earlier life period. If circumstances demand that these roles change, the ensuing conflict between new and old roles would precipitate a suicidal crisis in the family.

5. *Closed family system*: A suicidal family has a low tolerance for contacts outside the family system that could threaten to alter the established family structure.

6. *Aggression and death wishes directed against the potentially suicidal person by the family*: In suicidal families, there is a distinct pattern of hostility communicated both verbally and non-verbally to the suicidal individual. The suicidal individual is the recipient of the accumulated aggression of the family.

7. *Scapegoating*: This takes the form of the punitive isolation and alienation of the suicidal person from the rest of the family.

8. *Sadomasochistic relationships*: Members of suicidal families alternate between being hurt and hurting others.

9. *Double-bind relationships*: Members of the suicidal family are characterized by a "barbed wire exterior." Anyone coming close is hurt, yet no one can tolerate distance.

10. *Suicidal person is the "bad object" for the family*: In suicidal families, the suicidal individual is seen as acting out the forbidden wishes and bad impulses of other family members. The collective guilt over such impulses and wishes is then expiated through the suicidal act.

11. *Quality of family fragility*: A suicidal family regards itself as inadequate to meet the demands of everyday living.

12. *Family depression*: Suicidal families are often preoccupied with death and apprehensive over loss and annihilation of the self.

13. *Communication disturbances*: Suicidal families seem to be unaware or non-receptive to verbal messages from the suicidal family member. In general, the

family is characterized by a paucity of dialogue, a tendency towards rejection of mutual communication, and a critical attitude towards establishing communication outside the family system.

14. *Intolerance for crisis*: Suicidal families have no tolerance for a crisis which would affect the everyday pattern of family life.

Richman's investigation is significant because it supplements a naturalistic approach with concern for methodological rigor. Using a large sample of subjects and a control group of normal families, the study attempts to present a systematic and scientifically treated set of data without sacrificing the richness, depth, and complexity of the subject under examination. However, as the investigator himself admits, it is a difficult task to determine which patterns of family functioning are particular to families with a suicidal member and which are simply characteristic of emotionally disturbed families in general. A number of the patterns of family functioning which Richman identifies in his experimental group (e.g., scapegoating, double-bind communications, etc.) are also present in families in which there is a manifestation of psychosis, particularly schizophrenia in a family member. What than makes an individual within a pathological family system choose suicide instead of psychosis or some other form of pathological behavior?

One method of determining the answer to this question would be to conduct a comparative investigation of a variety of pathological family systems including those with a suicidal member with the explicit purpose of uncovering characteristics which might differentiate one system from another. While such a study is appealing, the thoughtful investigator must question the extent of the present knowledge and understanding of systems with a suicidal member and whether the existing theoretical and empirical model is adequately developed enough for submission to comparative study. A retrospective glance at the literature suggests that investigators have only begun to isolate and understand definitive characteristics of such systems. Even Richman's study, which attempts a broader and more encompassing description of family systems with a suicidal member, falls considerably short of presenting a well-integrated and organized picture of the components which make up these systems. It is likely that family systems with a suicidal member can be compared effectively to other pathological family systems only after they themselves have been more clearly defined and understood.

The present study investigated families with a suicidal member with two goals in mind. The first goal was to present a richer, more in-depth, and complete description of such systems; the second, to develop a more organized and integrated formulation about their nature. This inquiry focused specifically on families in which an adolescent member exhibited suicidal behavior. Suicidal behavior was defined as the communication of intent to hurt oneself either by written or verbal statement or by the actual act of attempting suicide.

The approach to this investigation followed three basic assumptions. These assumptions were instrumental in determining the major areas of focus for data collection. The first assumption concerns the relationship between the manifested symptom, in this case suicidal behavior, and the family system. The assumption contends that suicidal behavior is an expression of system malfunction and that, in addition, it serves in a functional capacity for the family. The area of focus derived from this assumption is that of understanding the significance of the suicidal behavior within the context of the family system. That is, what, if any, are the systemic precipitants of the behavior; what is the meaning of the behavior to the system as a whole; and what type of response and change, if any, occurs in the system as a result of the behavior. The second basic assumption which underlies this investigation stems from a consideration of the existing literature on suicide which posits a strong relationship between self-destruction and the phenomena of separation and loss. A review of the literature reveals that both theorists and empiricists have stressed the role of separation and loss in the understanding of suicidal ideation and behavior. Freud (1957) emphasized the loss of a love object; Durkheim (1951) stressed the loss of identification with a social group; Beck (1967), and Kobler and Stotland (1964) underline the loss of hope; Adam (1973) points to loss of or separation from parental figures in early childhood; Stengel (1958) stresses separation or loss within the context of a close emotional relationship; and Humphrey et al. (1974) suggest that loss of role within marital, occupational, or academic contexts, as well as loss of mental or physical health, can be instrumental in the precipitation of suicidal behavior. It is important to note that the literature cited here is only representative of a small portion of the speculations and findings of this type. There appears, then, to be a cross-theoretical and cross-empirical consensus that the issues of loss and separation are significant in the precipitation and understanding of self destruction. Consequently, the present study assumed that these issues would also be of significance for the family system with a suicidal member. Thus, the second area selected for focus is concerned with the occurrence and quality of issues of loss and separation in such family systems. The third basic assumption addresses general family style and contends that family systems, just like individuals, develop characteristic styles of coping with anxiety-laden issues and areas of conflict. Thus, the third area of focus centers on the extent and nature of the defensive, strategical, and maintenance styles of family systems with a suicidal member.

The present investigation integrated and formulated the data collected through the application of theoretical perspectives drawn from the work of three major systems theorists. The theoretical frameworks selected for inclusion in the study trace their roots to the basic notion underlying the systems paradigm, that is, that pathology is a manifestation of a problem in the family system and not simply a manifestation of a particular individual's difficulties. However, while these frameworks share this underlying assumption, they differ in their basic approach to the study of the family. The theoretical systems chosen for inclusion in this investigation were those of Bowen (1976), Nagy (1973), and Kantor (1975). The work of these three men represents historical-developmental, historical-phenomenologi-cal, and structural-phenomenological approaches to the family system, respectively.

The work of Bowen is an example of a systems-interactional approach that gives consideration to the role of historical-developmental antecedents in the formation of the malfunctioning family system. Bowen believes that "emotional illness is a far deeper process than can be explained by emotional trauma in a single generation" and he postulates that the psychopathology and malfunction man-ifested in a family system may be rooted generations back as well as extended to generations in the future.

Two major variables—level of anxiety and degree of integration of the emotional and intellectual capabilities of the self—underlie his approach. Bowen contends that individuals with a lower degree of integration of these capabilities are dominated by the "automatic emotional system" and as a result are less flexible, less adaptable, more emotionally dependent on others, and run a greater risk of developing emotional dysfunction in response to increasing levels of anxiety. Drawing on these variables, Bowen has created a number of constructs with which to understand the historical-developmental processes at work in the malfunction-ing family system. Those constructs which specifically address the manner in which various patterns of emotional functioning are perpetuated within and across generations of families include "the family projection process," "emotional cutoff," and "multigenerational transmission." Bowen proposes that the family projection process occurs in varying degrees within the immediate nuclear family depending upon both the level of anxiety and the degree of self-integration of the parents. If self-integration is low and anxiety is high, severe emotional impairment of one or more children is likely to occur. A second critical factor underlying this projection process is the emotional cutoff, or "the extent and manner in which individuals separate themselves from the past in order to start their lives in the present generation." The more abrupt the cutoff, or the more unresolved the emotional attachment to the past, the more probable is the perpetuation of emo-tional dysfunction in current and future generations. Bowen labels the perpetuation of such emotional dysfunction across generations the "multi-generational trans-mission process" and believes that the child who is the primary object of the family projection process becomes the vehicle through which unresolved family issues are passed on.

Nagy's approach to the family system is primarily an historical-phenomenological one. He subscribes to the notion of inter-generational influence in the patterning of family relationships and he contends that the quality of the "interlocking" or the interaction of individual intra-psychic processes and sys-temic or "multi-person" processes is the primary factor in the determination of pathology. Nagy's framework assumes an added dimensionality as he proposes an alternative to straight-line causation, or monothetical thinking which views pathology as determined by a cause or series of causes. Nagy's alternative is the dialectical approach which underscores what he calls the "dual psychic reality" of any relationship. He explains:

> The essence of the dialectical approach is a liberation of the mind from absolute concepts which in themselves claim to explain phenomena as though the opposite point of view did not exist. According to dialectical thought, a positive concept is always viewed in contrast with its opposite, in the hope that their joint consideration will yield a resolution through a more thorough and productive understanding.

Nagy views the individual as a partner in a continuous and constantly changing dialogue or dynamic exchange with his or her relational counterpart or Other. This on-going process of reciprocal self-definition bases the subjective experience of each individual in the relational interaction. In short, the dialectical approach "retains the individual as a center of his universe but views him in an ontologically dependent interaction with his constituitive other."

Nagy contends that the "inter-locking" of individual and systemic forces can only be viewed dialectically, i.e., consideration of one outside a context which includes the other is meaningless. His viewpoint emphasizes the dynamic nature of family homeostasis as he believes that "the prevalence of movement over stagnation is the essence of the dialectical view of family relationships." From Nagy's perspective, system equilibrium is continually influenced and necessarily changed by the actions of individual members. A disruption in system homeostasis results in a qualitative rebalancing or synthesis of the forces of change with the pre-existing state of the system. Thus, the individual members and the system as a whole may be regarded as participants in an on-going dialogue in which their opposite or antithetical contributions effect systemic change and redefinition.

Kantor approaches the study of the family system using a structural-phenomenological framework. He develops a highly complex and specific set of constructs to facilitate insight into the relational realities experienced by family members in their day-to-day lives. In general, Kantor views families as open, adaptive, information processing systems that are purposive and goal-seeking in nature. All activity between or among members of the system is seen as interdependent, or "interactional." For Kantor, interaction pertaining to the family system always occurs within specific fields of shared experience. He divides such fields or dimensions into two categories. Physical fields or "access dimensions" (i.e., Space, Time, and Energy) include the quantitative or physical means through which family members actualize their search for experience. Conceptual fields or "target dimensions" (i.e., Meaning, Affect, and Power) encompass the qualitative or conceptual means through which the life goals of family members are thematically actualized. Recuring patterns of interactional sequences which take place within these dimensions are "evolved by the persons in that field to regulate and shape the relationships between and among themselves." Thus, broadly speaking, Kantor conceptualizes family systems from within a distance regulational model which emphasizes the attainment of family goals through the repeated regulation of distance among family members and between family members and events.

Using these combined theoretical perspectives to study family systems in which an adolescent member had exhibited suicidal behavior provided a rich conceptual framework with which to understand the data without sacrificing or placing limits on the meaning which the data itself had to offer.

2

The Methodological Approach

The Sample

Originally, at least five and no fewer than three families in which an adolescent family member had exhibited suicidal behavior were to be studied. The sample was to be as homogeneous as possible with regard to the following criteria: 1) socio-economic status; 2) religious-ethnic background; 3) sex and age of the suicidal family member; 4) suicidal member's residence at home at the time of the exhibited suicidal behavior; and 5) home conditions in which both parents were alive and residing together.

In pursuing the location of a sample that met these criteria, a number of problems became readily apparent. Due to the highly sensitive nature of the material and its inherent tendency to raise moral and legal issues, as well as the planned unconventional approach to the data collection and analysis, institutions that might have helped to recruit families balked and would not participate. Eventually, a working relationship was established with two mental health facilities in the area that speculated that in a few months time they could provide the needed families. However, after a considerable length of time, data were collected from only one family who met the criteria. This long delay made clear additional problems regarding the location of an appropriate sample. Although there were adolescents at both facilities who had exhibited suicidal behavior and were willing to participate in the study, they were eliminated most often by the existing criteria, particularly the requirements that the family be intact and that the suicidal member be residing at home at the time of the suicidal behavior. Furthermore, "intact" families were unwilling to participate because they feared an invasion of their privacy. After carefully reviewing the situation and possible alternative approaches, it was decided that instead of interviewing whole families, only the suicidal adolescent would be interviewed although the investigation would still keep a family-oriented perspective. Criteria were revised to include subjects of either sex between the ages of 13 and 19 who had exhibited suicidal behavior. Residence at home at the time of the behavior and an intact family were preferable qualifications but were no longer required for participation in the study. The goal was to collect data from no fewer than five adolescent subjects.

Even with these less stringent criteria locating appropriate subjects was difficult and time consuming. Many of the adolescents who qualified for the study proved unreliable; they would agree to participate and later not follow through with the commitment. However, after four months elapsed, data had been collected from six adolescent subjects. This data as well as the data collected earlier from the one participating family constituted the final sample. The following chapters present case material from the one participating family and two of the six adolescent participants.

Interview Schedules

Two interview schedules—one for the interviews with the participating family and one for the interviews with the single adolescents—were used in the inquiry. Both schedules derived their basic format from the three general focal areas outlined earlier: 1) occurrence and quality of loss and separation; 2) general family maintenance, defensive, and coping styles; and 3) suicidal behavior—response and function. Initially, these focal areas were divided into categories which were representative of the salient aspects of each (table 1). Specific interview questions were then developed to facilitate a discussion of these points and to prompt a descriptive narrative, the substance of which would be qualitative and experiential. Following this approach, an interview schedule was designed for use with families (table 2). This schedule included interviews with individual family members, the parents, and the entire family. Individual interviews created an atmosphere in which participants might feel freer to present their own viewpoints and experiences, while group interviews provided the opportunity to observe family members communicate and interact with one another.

The decision to shift from interviewing entire families to interviewing single adolescents altered certain aspects of the interview process. It eliminated the chance to get to know the adolescent's family first hand (i.e., observing family interaction directly and forming direct impressions of family members). In addition, the quantity and quality of historical and current information about the family was correspondingly limited. However, it did offer the possibility of a more in-depth examination of the adolescents themselves. The interview schedule was adapted to compensate for these changes (table 3). Questions directed at specific family members were replaced with questions designed to encourage the adolescent to share his or her perceptions of other family members and of family interaction. Questions aimed at uncovering information most likely unavailable to the adolescent, such as specifics about the parents' families of origins, were deemphasized, while new topics such as dreams and the experience of becoming

Table 1. Areas of Focus

I. Loss and Separation
    A. History and quality (e.g., temporary-permanent, intrapersonal-interpersonal, material etc.)
        1. In parents' families of origin
        2. In marriage before birth of children
        3. In present family
    B. Expectations
        1. Expectant attitudes about loss and separation
            a) In parents' families of origin
            b) In marriage before the birth of the children
            c) In present family
        2. Expectations about behaviors and feelings that may lead to loss and separation
            a) In parents' families of origin
            b) In marriage before birth of the children
            c) In present family
    C. Perception and understanding of the process
        1. In parents' families of origin
        2. In marriage before birth of children
        3. In present family
    D. Coping styles: behaviors and feelings
        1. In parents' families of origin
        2. In marriage before birth of children
        3. In present family
II. General Family Coping Style
    A. Goals and values of family
        1. In marriage before birth of children
        2. In present family
    B. Family rules (i.e., what is and is not permissible in the family)
    C. Decision-making processes
        1. In marriage
        2. In entire family
    D. Resolution of conflict
        1. In marriage
        2. In entire family
        3. With the suicidal member
    E. Sources of support
        1. Inside the family
        2. Outside the family
III. Suicidal behavior: Response and Function
    A. Current and past suicidal behavior(s)
        1. Circumstances
        2. Immediate response of family members
        3. Perception and understanding of behavior (s) by family members
    B. Changes in family around behavior(s)
        1. Feelings
        2. Events
        3. Expectations for future

Table 2. Family Interview Schedule

Interview #1: Introduction
- A. Introduce myself—background and credentials
- B. Reasons for the study
- C. Describe study
  1. Number of hours
  2. Schedule of interviews
  3. Interview process
- D. Explain taping and confidentiality
- E. Answer questions
- F. Gather demographic data
- G. Arrange next interview

Interview #2: Husband and Wife
- A. How they met and why they chose one another
  1. Circumstances surrounding courtship and decision to marry
     - a) Living situation at time: living at or away from home?
     - b) Work/education situation
     - c) What feelings, events, etc. were influential in their decision to marry at that point in their personal development?
     - d) How did their respective parents feel about the courtship and marriage?
     - e) What were their expectations of marriage and each other?
  2. Shared goals and values (what did they have in common; how were they different?)
     - a) Education
     - b) Financial/professional
     - c) Social/religious
     - d) Personal
     - e) Future
- B. Development of the marital relationship before the birth of children with regard to . . .
  1. Role of separation and loss
     - a) Were there any significant experiences of loss and separation?
       - (1) Work
       - (2) Education
       - (3) Social life
       - (4) Material
       - (5) Other
     - b) Were these separations and/or losses anticipated?
     - c) What was their meaning to and effect on the marital relationship?
     - d) How were they handled?
       - (1) Resources within the marriage
       - (2) Resources outside the marriage
         - (a) Friends
         - (b) Family
         - (c) Professional help
         - (d) Other
  2. Coping Styles
     - a) How is the marriage structured, that is, what are the rules, who is allowed to do what?
     - b) How did they make decisions?
     - c) Disagreements

Table 2. Continued

Interviews 3-4: Individual Parent

           (1)   About what?

           (2)   How were they resolved?

A.   Family background

    1.   When growing up did they experience any significant separations or losses?

        a)   Significant other(s)

           (1)   Inside family (immediate or extended family)

           (2)   Outside family

        b)   Other types of separation or loss

    2.   Were these separations and/or losses anticipated?

    3.   How did you and your family cope with the separations and/or losses?

    4.   Were these separations and/or losses explained to you?

        a)   By whom?

        b)   In what manner?

        c)   How did you understand and feel about separations and/or losses after explanation?

    5.   Did your family experience any incidents of separation and/or loss involving you?

        a)   Were they anticipated?

        b)   How were they explained and understood?

        c)   How did you and the family feel about and cope with these incidents?

B.   Current life situations

    1.   What are your goals?

        a)   Work or professional life

        b)   Interpersonal relations, social life

    2.   What resources or sources of support do you have?

        a)   Inside family (nuclear, extended)

        b)   Outside family (work, social, etc.)

C.   Perceptions of suicidal member

    1.   What was the suicidal member like as a child?

    2.   Do you perceive him/her in the same way now?

    3.   What were the critical incidents in his/her development?

    4.   If there are other children, how, if at all, is the suicidal member different?

D.   Expectations of the future

    1.   Regarding family

        a)   Spouse/marriage

        b)   Suicidal member

        c)   Other children

    2.   Other goals, plans, hopes

Interview #5: Husband and Wife

A.   Experiences of loss and/or separation since the birth of the children including those experiences involving the children

    1.   History and quality

    2.   Were they anticipated?

    3.   Did they explain them to the children; if so, how?

    4.   What was their meaning to the parents and other family members?

    5.   How did the parents/rest of the family respond; how did they cope with these incidents?

    6.   Were there ensuing changes in the marital relationship around these incidents?

B.   Current relationship with the children

Table 2. Continued

      1. Suicidal member

      2. Other children

  C. Changes in marital relationships since birth of the children

      1. Goals and values

      2. Feelings towards one another

      3. Decision-making processes

      4. Incidents of conflict and their resolutions

  D. Relationships outside the family

      1. Work

      2. Social

      3. Other

Interview #6: Suicidal Family Member

  A. His/her experience with loss and/or separation

      1. History and quality

      2. Were they anticipated?

      3. Were they explained to you, if so, by whom?

      4. How did you understand them?

      5. How did you cope with them?

  B. Role in family decision-making process

      1. Are you included in the process?

      2. When/how often?

      3. How?

  C. Role with regard to family conflicts and conflict resolution

      1. Are you ever the center of conflict in the family?

         a) When/how often?

         b) What type of conflict?

         c) With whom?

      2. How are these conflicts resolved?

  D. Perceptions of self/parents/siblings

      1. How would you describe yourself?

      2. How would you describe your parents?

      3. How would you describe your siblings?

  E. Suicidal behavior

      1. How do you understand it?

      2. How would you explain it to other family members?

      3. What would change in your family if your attempt had been successful?

  F. Sources of support

      1. Inside family—is there anyone in the family that you can turn to for support?

         a) Who?

         b) Under what circumstances?

         c) How often?

         d) Are they helpful; if so, how?

      2. Outside family

         a) Who?

         b) Under what circumstances?

         c) How often?

         d) Are they helpful; if so, how?

Interview #7: Parents and Suicidal Member

  A. Suicide attempt(s)

Table 2. Continued

---

    1. Circumstances surrounding attempt(s)
        a) How, where, when?
        b) Family events preceding attempt(s)
            (1) Areas of conflict being dealt with
            (2) Decisions being made
        c) Where were other family members at the time of the attempt(s)?
        d) What were their immediate reactions?
            (1) Feelings
            (2) Behaviors
    2. Was the attempt(s) anticipated?
    3. How was the attempt(s) understood; explained to other family members?
    4. If there was more than one attempt, were the attempts similar?
        a) Nature
        b) Circumstances
 B. Change in family after suicide attempt(s)
    1. Relationships between various family members
        a) As sources of support
        b) As conflict-laden
    2. Relationships with extended family and people outside family
    3. Other events or circumstances involving change

---

an adolescent were introduced to provide the adolescent with more of an opportunity to elaborate on his or her own experiences.

Collecting the Data

In order to locate subjects, the clinical staff at the two participating mental health facilities were asked to review their case load for clients who met the stated criteria. Therapists with suitable clients were then asked to decide on the appropriateness of discussing involvement in the study with the client and his or her family. If the individuals approached agreed to participate, they were contacted to make the necessary arrangements for the interview procedure. All participants were given an Informed Consent Statement to sign.

Subjects were interviewed in their homes or at the participating mental health facilities. All interview sessions were taped on a cassette recorder with the subject's permission. Interview sessions with the one participating family lasted between 2-3 hours and a total of 12 hours of tape recorded material was collected. Interview sessions with the single adolescents ranged from 1-3 hours in length and a total of 18 hours of tape recorded material was collected. Subjects were permitted to listen to the tapes at the completion of the inquiry and to share the material with their respective therapists if they requested to do so. Only one of the subjects chose to listen to her interview sessions at the completion of the inquiry. A complete transcription of the family interview sessions and summaries and partial transcriptions of the single adolescent interviews were completed by the interviewer.

Table 3. Single Adolescent Interview Schedule

A. Experience with loss and separation
  1. History and quality
  2. Were they anticipated?
  3. Were they explained to you? By whom?
  4. How did you understand them?
  5. How did you cope with them?
  6. How did others in your family understand them and cope with them?
  7. Can you think of any losses/separations that you did not experience but which were significant for other family members?
B. Perception of self and family
  1. Describe yourself
  2. Describe your parents
  3. Describe your siblings and/or other important family members such as extended family
  4. Describe your relationship with each of the other members in your family
  5. Describe the relationship between your parents
  6. Describe the relationship between each of your parents and other family members
  7. Who are you most like in your family? How and why?
  8. Who are you closest to in your family and why?
  9. Who are you least close to and why?
  10. Describe close relationships between or among other members of your family
  11. Who gets along best with whom?
  12. Which family members do not get along with each other?
  13. Who can you turn to for support?
      a) Inside the family
      b) Outside the family
  14. Under what type of circumstances do you seek support? How often?
  15. Is the support helpful? If so, how?
C. Role in family decision-making process
  1. Who makes the decisions in your family?
  2. Are you ever included? If so, how, how often, and when?
D. Role with regard to family conflicts and conflict resolution
  1. What are the major conflicts in your family; that is, what do they argue about most?
  2. Who argues with whom?
  3. With whom do you argue ?
  4. Are you ever the center of a conflict or an argument in your family? If so, when, how often, with whom, and what type of conflict is involved?
  5. How do family members resolve conflicts or arguments?
  6. How do you resolve conflicts or arguments?
E. Suicidal Behavior
  1. Describe suicidal behavior(s)
  2. Circumstances surrounding behavior(s)
      a) Location of yourself and other family members
      b) Events in or outside the family preceding the behavior(s)
      c) Decisions being made (personal, social, or within the family)
      d) Areas of conflict being dealt with within the family context or environment at large
  3. Effect of behavior(s) on your family
      a) Were the behavior(s) anticipated?
      b) How were they explained within and outside the family?

Table 3. Continued

---

      c) How do you think family members understood them?
      d) How did they cope with them?
      e) General reactions inside and outside the family context

  4. Your experience of the behavior(s)
      a) How did you understand your behavior? Do you understand it differently now?
      b) How would you explain it to other family members?
      c) How would you explain it to people outside the immediate family?

  5. Changes as a result of your behavior(s)
      a) Changes between yourself and other family members (i.e., in relationships)
      b) Changes between other family members (i.e., in relationships)
      c) Changes in your relationships with people outside of the immediate family
      d) Other events or circumstances of change
      e) What if anything would change in your family if your suicidal behavior had been successful?

  6. Influence of others regarding your suicidal behavior(s)
      a) Do you know of other people either inside or outside your family that have engaged in suicidal behavior(s)?
          (1) Who?
          (2) Describe the behavior(s)
          (3) Do you consider these behaviors similar to your own? If so, how?
          (4) Did the suicidal behavior (s) of others influence your decision to behave suicidally? If so, how?

F. Dreams
  1. Do you remember your dreams?
  2. If so, which dreams stand out in your mind? Describe them
  3. Have you ever had repetitive dreams? If so, describe them
  4. Do you remember dreaming before or after your suicidal behavior(s)? If so, about what? Do you feel that any of these dreams were related to your suicidal behavior(s)?
  5. How do you understand your dreams; that is, what do they mean to you?

G. Experience of becoming an adolescent
  1. Do you remember what it was like to become a teenager?
  2. Did your family treat you differently? If so, how?
  3. Did you find yourself spending your time differently? If so, how, where and with whom?
  4. Did things change at home? If so, how and when did you notice the change?

H. The Future
  1. What do you see in your future?
  2. What are your goals for the future?
  3. How will you go about attaining your goals?

Identifying data on all participants have been changed in order to insure confidentiality.

Presentation and Analysis of the Interview Material

Current and background information about all the subjects will be presented in a case history format. The purpose of this presentation is to acquaint the reader with the study's participants and to provide a descriptive foundation for the discussion to follow. Because of the theoretical importance of the role played by experiences of loss and separation in understanding the data, the case histories were constructed with particular emphasis on these experiences in the lives of the subjects.

The body of each case history is organized to facilitate a broad understanding of the development of the family system—its origins, the manner in which it has progressed, and its current status. After a brief introduction of identifying data, each case history offers a summary of the available parental history. In the case of the one participating family, this section is followed by a developmental description of the current family, beginning with the courtship of the spouses and concluding with the family as it exists at present. A brief description of salient family interaction is also included. For the single adolescents, the available parental history is followed by an account of personal and family history from the participant's birth to the present. All case histories conclude with a description of the personal characteristics of the participants and of the interview process in general. These descriptions are based on both the impressions of the interviewer and statements made by the participants about themselves and, in the case of the family, about each other.

Due to the exploratory nature of the study and the variable nature of the data collection, it was difficult to predict the exact form that the data analysis would take. Optimally, it was to include the content of responses to questions, the interviewer's impressions of subjects, and, when available, the interviewer's sense of the family interaction. The inquiry was undertaken within a format that would lend a basic structure to the data while allowing the data to assume its own direction within that structure relatively unencumbered by preconceived notions about its meaning or form. To review, three focal areas—1) occurrence and quality of events of separation and loss; 2) general family maintenance, defensive, and coping styles; and 3) suicidal behavior (response and function)—constituted the minimal foundation for the data collection. Because of the open-ended nature of the project and the abundant and varied information collected, it seemed sensible to approach the data analysis initially through these established areas of focus. In so doing, temporary themes surfaced, but seemed disconnected. Many parts appeared to be present, but a total "gestalt" did not emerge. Frequent attempts were made to abandon the three focal perspectives to examine the data without these constructs. These attempts met with periodic success, but at times they resulted in even more fragmentation of the material. However, ultimately, two particular areas remained in the foreground regardless of the approach that the analysis assumed. Incidents of separation and loss and the adolescents' suicidal behavior seemed to call consistently for examination. Eventually, the focus shifted entirely to the area of loss and separation, while the specific accounts of suicidal behavior were temporarily shelved. In retrospect, it would seem to be more than the particular biases and interests of the researcher that elevated this material to a special place. Rather, it appeared that loss and separation played a strikingly important role in the lives of those involved in the inquiry. From the dimension of loss and separation, a consistent and powerful set of themes emerged that seemed to dominate the material as well as to lend a great deal of clarity to the understanding of some salient aspects of family functioning. The more that various aspects of loss and separation were examined, the more a systemic configuration surfaced in the data suggesting a relationship between numerous components of family functioning and an adolescent's suicidal behavior.

The following analysis attempts to present an outline of this configuration. It simplifies what appear to be inherent relationships as much as possible in order to underscore and enhance dominant and significant themes without sacrificing the richness of the data or the depth of the configuration itself. Of course, the parts of this configuration cannot be considered mutually exclusive; however, they are presented for discussion as separate entities with the hope that this approach will lend clarity to their comprehension. As these components are presented and discussed consecutively, their interdependent relationship will become clear.

The order in which the components are presented was dictated by the conceptual process which gave birth to the configuration itself. Four configurational components will be presented for discussion in chapters 4, 5, and 6. The first involves what has emerged as the highly significant area of loss and separation. Specifically, chapter 4 is a descriptive presentation of the affective and cognitive associations to past and current incidents of loss and separation made by both individuals and families. It examines how individuals feel and think about loss and separation and attempts to uncover the shared meanings and affects attributed to these events both within and across generations. The second component is presented in chapter 5 and is concerned with the delineation of relational patterns in family systems that have specific cognitive and affective associations to loss and separation. That is, how does the manner in which loss and separation are experienced by family members influence the way in which they form relationships between and among themselves. The third and fourth components are the focus of discussion in chapter 6. The third component addresses itself to an examination of the configuration of family relationships within the context of meaning. Given that the relational patterns have been identified, what is their ultimate purpose? Why, specifically, are these relational configurations important in the insurance of family functioning? Finally, the fourth component examines adolescent suicidal behavior as it reflects both important elements of the structural and purposive aspects of these family systems.

The data collected from both the participating family and the original six adolescent participants were instrumental in the development of the theoretical configuration alluded to above. The material gathered from the family provides richer, more extensive information with which to illustrate major points; it will be utilized as a primary data source in the discussion of the model. Data gathered from two of the six adolescents will be included at relevant points in the discussion to provide additional support for the ideas generated.

3

The Families

The Balasco Family

Identifying Data

The Balascos are a middle class family who sold their home of eight years, three months prior to the interview, and bought and moved into a house in an adjacent New England community. This was the third move for the Balascos in 23 years of marriage.

Benjamin Balasco, age 52, works as a correctional officer at a local facility for federal, state, and county prisoners and is the family's primary source of financial support. Marie Balasco, age 46, obtained her high school degree three years ago and had recently begun work as a nurse's aid. Of the three Balasco children, the two boys, Teddy, age 16, and Davy, age 14, live at home and attend public high school. The oldest, daughter Christine, age 22, is married with a young child, works as a nurse, and lives with her family in the Balascos' former house.

The Balasco family is of Irish and Portuguese descent and numerous members of the extended family—aunts, uncles, and cousins— live in adjacent communities. Both sets of grandparents are deceased. Mr. and Mrs. Balasco were raised in the Catholic religion, but converted to Protestantism after the birth of their second child.

Several months prior to this inquiry, the Balascos' youngest child, Davy, wrote, at different intervals, three notes of a suicidal nature which Mrs. Balasco discovered while cleaning his room. However, prior to this writing and discovery of the notes, Davy's behaviors had been a source of conflict in the family and the Balascos had found it difficult to understand and manage Davy's staying out of the home late, his skipping school, and his choice of friends whom they felt were inappropriate and a bad influence on him. These behaviors compounded by the first suicidal note resulted in the Balascos seeking professional help for Davy at a local mental health facility. Dissatisfied with this facility's recommendation that Davy be hospitalized, the Balascos sought treatment for him at another psychiatric agency. It was during the course of treatment at the second agency that the remaining suicidal notes were written. The Balascos and Davy attended both family and individual therapy sessions for five months, and it was during this period that they came to the author's attention as being potentially appropriate for this inquiry. However, by the time arrangements with the Balasco family had been negotiated, Davy had chosen to terminate his contact with the mental health facility. Consequently, the Balasco family was not in treatment at the time that the interviews were conducted.

Available Parental History

Father's history: A personal account. Mr. Balasco was born in 1925 in a neighboring community, the ninth of 11 children of a Portuguese immigrant farmer and his wife. Figure 1 is a genogram of Mr. Balasco's family of origin. Prior to his birth, the Balasco family lost two of their children. Michael and Paul, born one and two years before Mr. Balasco respectively, died of black diphtheria. Shortly after Mr. Balasco's birth, he contracted the disease, became quite ill and the family anticipated a third death; however, unlike his brothers, Mr. Balasco did not succumb to the disease.

Describing his growing up, Mr. Balasco says of his place on the farm and in the family.

> It was strictly like we were institutionalized or in the service military-wise . . . not like these people didn't show love and affection . . . but they didn't have time for this . . . you know in the Depression days everything was meant to either make money or to work for the institution.

All of the Balasco children were born on the farm. Mr. Balasco remembers being told regarding his own birth that his mother worked in the fields all morning, delivered him in the afternoon, and was up washing her clothes in the evening. Mr. Balasco characterized both parents as authoritarian although his father more so. Of his father, Mr. Balasco recalls, "If he had anything to say, you were called into a room and he would say it . . . of course it wasn't always nice, but you got the message. The next time you would be on the ground looking up." Of his mother, Mr. Balasco has more mixed memories. He stated at one point that his mother "had a real way of coming on . . . you know she was a real wonderful person . . . she had a way of talking to you that made you feel that you were a part of her." However, at other times he commented that although they were close, they "were never that affectionate toward one another." In terms of discipline, he remembers both parents as being equally strict and states that neither dominated more when it came to disciplinary issues. ". . . you couldn't infiltrate the organization . . . they had their stuff together."

Mr. Balasco noted that there were many hardships while growing up. Although the children went to school, excessive amounts of work on the farm left

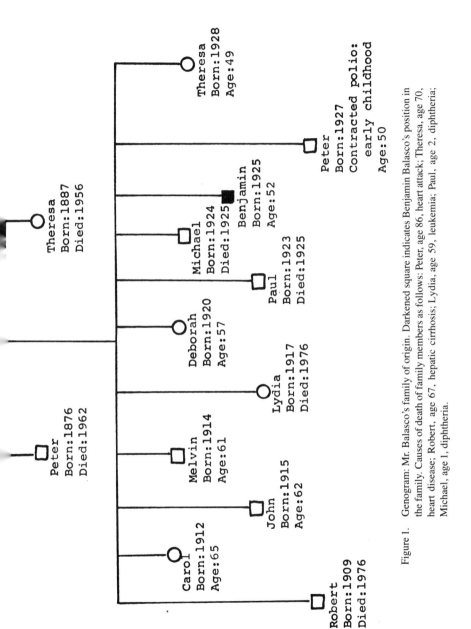

Figure 1. Genogram: Mr. Balasco's family of origin. Darkened square indicates Benjamin Balasco's position in the family. Causes of death of family members as follows: Peter, age 86, heart attack; Theresa, age 70, heart disease; Robert, age 67, hepatic cirrhosis; Lydia, age 59, leukemia; Paul, age 2, diphtheria; Michael, age 1, diphtheria.

little time for friends or activities outside the family sphere and even visits to nearby relatives were few as the family rarely left the farm. "Killing" (i.e., the slaughter of animals and the harvesting of crops) was another daily aspect of farm living that Mr. Balasco recollects feeling "pretty bad" about. Looking back he recalls, "it was kind of sad, seeing something produce so well that you have to kill it."

When Mr. Balasco was eight, the family experienced a loss as well as a major disappointment. The oldest boy, Robert, left home to pursue graduate studies and an eventual career in South America as a linguist. Robert's educational and professional choice contradicted the ethnic tradition of the family with its explicit expectation that the oldest boy become a lawyer, a priest, or a judge. In addition, his choice countered a more implicit expectation that the oldest son choose to be near home and to ultimately assume responsibility for the family. Mr. Balasco recalls Robert's choice and leavetaking as being quite difficult for his parents. Although he himself denies being affected by it, Mr. Balasco remembers his parents crying both at home and seeing Robert off at the train station. Several years later, Mr. Balasco's father was to turn the farm over to Robert. However, according to Mr. Balasco, Robert became an alcoholic who never assumed any responsibility for running the farm.

Shortly after Robert's departure, Carol, the oldest girl, left to marry an Irishman, an act that was "almost against the Portuguese dynasty . . . but my father overruled that because he (Carol's husband) was the type of guy that used to pitch in around the farm." Brother John was to follow soon after because of a disagreement with his father. Mr. Balasco remembers that John wanted to "play ball in the afternoon with the fellows" and his father said "milk the cows" at which point John refused and his father "showed him the door." John subsequently went to work on another farm where he could make money for working. In retrospect, Mr. Balasco notes, "The reason that we all left was to make a better life for ourselves even if it was farming we were going to get paid." Sisters Lydia and Deborah left the family to marry cousins and Mr. Balasco's brother Melvin moved from home to work at a General Electric plant because "everybody was too broke." Mr. Balasco states that when most of the kids left, the farm deteriorated significantly. A few years later, Mr. Balasco, feeling that he needed "to get away," enlisted in the Navy, an experience he was to enjoy because of the opportunity for travel as well as the fact that he was accustomed to the regimented structure of the service from the time that he had spent on the farm. After nine years in the Navy, Mr. Balasco decided to return home permanently, refusing a promotion in rank and job. Thinking back, Mr. Balasco considers his decision an unfortunate one. The only two siblings left on the farm were brother Peter, handicapped because of a childhood bout with polio, and sister Theresa who was as yet unmarried. Mr. Balasco recalls,

The farm had dwindled . . . the cows had gone to nothing . . . in some of the years I don't think that some of the stuff had moved . . . pieces of equipment were all in the fields and I saw it and I said I gotta get this thing back . . . it was the craziest thing that I ever did to come back.

Shortly after he returned, Mr. Balasco married a neighborhood girl and the two lived in a nearby apartment while Mr. Balasco worked for "practically nothing" on the farm. Roughly a year and a half after his marriage, Mr. Balasco separated from his wife and baby girl. Five years later, Mr. Balasco and his wife were divorced. In retrospect, Mr. Balasco blames the split on the poor living that he made on the farm and the couple's subsequent lack of money. According to Mr. Balasco, his wife went to work on another farm to bring in more money and adopted an "independent" attitude with which he found it difficult to live. Through the period of his marriage and part of his separation, Mr. Balasco stuck it out on the farm, hoping that his father would pay higher wages and hoping to shape the farm into its original productive state. However, after three years and a major disagreement between father and son over the sharing of the income that the crops brought in, Mr. Balasco left the farm and went to work at a local state mental hospital. Mr. Balasco recalls that his father was "despondent" about his leaving the farm and consequently he returned to "work around the farm" a couple of days a week until after his second marriage five years later.

Mother's history: A personal account. Mrs. Balasco is a native of the area in which she presently lives. She was born in 1931, the fifth of eight children, to working class Irish parents. Figure 2 is a genogram of Mrs. Balasco's family of origin. Mrs. Balasco's father was employed with the interstate railroad; her mother was the primary caretaker for the children in the home. When seven months pregnant with Mrs. Balasco, her mother as well as the rest of the family suffered a loss. While opening the gate from the house to the street to hail an ice cream truck, the oldest boy, Alan, age four, was struck and killed when the truck accidently careened up on the curve. Shortly after, Mrs. Balasco was born two months prematurely and, as a result, required hospitalization postnatally for two months due to her low birth weight (two lbs.) and difficulties with her digestive system. As she grew older, Mrs. Balasco recalls that the family frequently talked about her dead brother "like he was an angel" and she has always assumed that "he must have been a truly beautiful child." In retrospect, Mrs. Balasco speculates that both her parents felt guilty about the incident, her mother simply for allowing Alan out in the yard and her father for not accompanying his son to the ice cream truck as was his usual habit.

Generally, Mrs. Balasco remembers her family as a "close" one and suggests that this may have been due to the amount of illness present in the family from very early on. Mrs. Balasco's older sister, Evelyn, was born blind and deaf, never

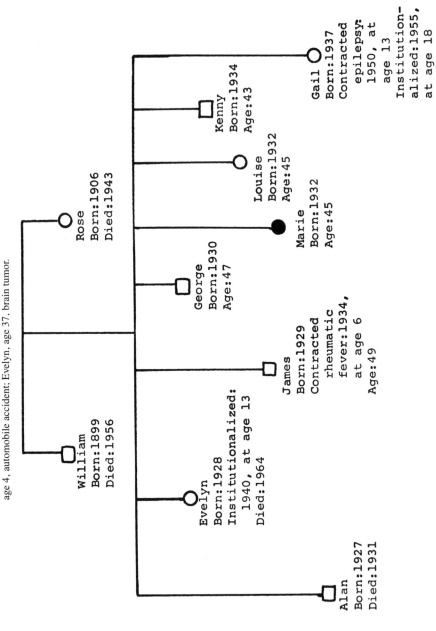

Figure 2. Genogram: Mrs. Balasco's family of origin. Darkened circle indicates Marie Balasco's position in the family. Causes of death as follows: Rose, age 37, pernicious anemia; William, age 57, cancer; Alan, age 4, automobile accident; Evelyn, age 37, brain tumor.

William
Born:1899
Died:1956

Rose
Born:1906
Died:1943

Evelyn
Born:1928
Institutionalized:
1940, at age 13
Died:1964

James
Born:1929
Contracted
rheumatic
fever:1934,
at age 6
Age:49

George
Born:1930
Age:47

Marie
Born:1932
Age:45

Louise
Born:1932
Age:45

Kenny
Born:1934
Age:43

Gail
Born:1937
Contracted
epilepsy:
1950, at
age 13
Institution-
alized:1955,
at age 18

Alan
Born:1927
Died:1931

developed speech, and eventually was diagnosed as having a brain tumor. Mrs. Balasco recollects sticking by Evelyn, "leading" her and playing with her. A second sibling, Jimmy, also demanded attention when at six years of age he contracted rheumatic fever and was hospitalized several times over the next years because of the subsequent development of a heart murmur. Although she would have been only three or four years old at the time Jimmy was initially ill, Mrs. Balasco states that she remembers taking care of the family when her mother went to the city to visit Jimmy in the hospital. When Jimmy did return home he was bedridden, a situation which placed severe restrictions on his activity level, as well as the activity level of the other children at home who were not allowed to "play rough with him or to make noise in the house."

Mrs. Balasco remembers her parents during these years as "good living people" who "really kind of lived for each other." She describes her mother as " a very soft woman . . . understanding and very compassionate." She recollects her father as "a mild man" who "wasn't really affectionate like my mother" but who "had a lot of compassion when we were sick." Mrs. Balasco's father worked an erratic schedule and was often unable to spend much time with the family. Mrs. Balasco remembers her only other older sibling, George, as being the family favorite because he was "bright and witty" in addition to being physically healthy. Mrs. Balasco admits to feeling closest to George because "we had a lot of chores in common" and states that he always was "protective" of her. Family life at that time seemed to be centered around the house. Mrs. Balasco recalls that her mother always kept the children close by . . inventing pasttimes to keep them "contented at home." Mrs. Balasco noted, "She never really let us go out a lot on our own."

The family endured a major separation when Evelyn, aged 13, was sent to a local state hospital after Mrs. Balasco's parents decided that they could no longer give her adequate care at home. Evelyn was to remain there until she died at age 37. Mrs. Balasco remembers the family missing Evelyn and always making gifts to send to her. As Mrs. Balasco grew older, she and her siblings were taken by their father to visit Evelyn.

The event which seems to have affected Mrs. Balasco the most during her childhood was the sudden death of her mother when she was 12 years old. Mrs. Balasco's mother, age 37 at the time, presented with "flu-like" symptoms, was taken to the hospital, and died a few days later of what Mrs. Balasco recalls to be a diagnosis of pernicious anemia. Mrs. Balasco remembers her father coming home, telling the children that their mother had died, and saying to her "get the kids cleaned up." Mrs. Balasco had difficulty recollecting how her siblings reacted to the news. She remembers the death being difficult for her to fully comprehend because she "was so young." Family members kept their feelings about the death to themselves and Mrs. Balasco turned to a teacher at school and to the church for emotional support. Prior to the funeral, the family split up with many of the children going to stay with relatives temporarily, until after the burial. Only Mrs.

Balasco, her brother George, and her sister Louise remained at home. Mrs. Balasco was the one child who accompanied her father to the funeral service.

Approximately two months after her mother's death, Mrs. Balasco began to suffer from severe stomach aches. Medical attention revealed a serious ulcer condition that was to present Mrs. Balasco with difficulties all through her life. For a number of years following their mother's death, Mrs. Balasco and her brother George assumed major household responsibilities including care of the other children. Mrs. Balasco remembers cooking and washing in addition to working after school as a waitress to bolster the family's deteriorating financial situation. When Mrs. Balasco was 15, her brother George left home to enter the service. She recalls feeling bad but states, "I suppose he felt that he had to get away." Mrs. Balasco carried on with her responsibilities at home and eventually dropped out of high school at age 17½ when all the work became too much. The number of family members living at home began to diminish further as brother Jimmy had gone to live permanently with an aunt and sister Louise left home to work as a live-in housekeeper in a nearby community. Left at home were Mrs. Balasco, her father, and her younger siblings, Kenny and Gail. Due to a change in ownership, the family was evicted from their home of 13 years and Mrs. Balasco took the opportunity to move in with a friend and get a job, although her actions contradicted her father's wish that she remain and care for the family. The family was further fragmented when Gail moved in with friends of the family. Around this time, Mrs. Balasco met and married a "nice boy" her age because she still felt that "Gail and Kenny needed somebody." Gail subsequently came to live with the newlyweds. Mrs. Balasco describes her relationship with her husband in "brother-sister" terms. The couple was married for two years and never consummated the marriage. In retrospect, Mrs. Balasco admits, "I didn't even know where babies came from." During the course of marital and sexual counseling with her local church representative, Mrs. Balasco learned that, contrary to her own wishes, her husband did not want to have children. An annulment was suggested and two years later, Mrs. Balasco followed through with this course of action. Mr. Balasco recalls no hard feelings between herself and her husband. After the annulment, Mrs. Balasco lived with her sister Gail and took a job at a local state mental hospital where she would eventually meet Mr. Balasco.

Current Family History: The Family's Perspective

Mr. and Mrs. Balasco were both financially independent, living on their own and working at the state mental hospital when they met in 1952. Both agree that their relationship, which was to grow more serious over the following two years, was the primary factor that motivated them to seek permanent separations from their respective spouses. Mrs. Balasco states that she was attracted to her second husband because, "He was a hard worker, honest, giving, and caring . . . like a diamond in the rough." Mr. Balasco recalls being drawn to his second wife because she was "easy-going, artistic, and neat and clean." Both Mr. and Mrs. Balasco describe their social life as minimal but adequate during courtship and after marriage. The Balascos' decision to marry was highly approved of by their respective parents. Coinciding with their marriage in 1954 was the purchase of a large house roughly one and one-half miles from the farm home of Mr. Balasco's parents. Mrs. Balasco's youngest sister, Gail, lived with the couple during the first one and one-half years of their married life. However, Gail suffered from an epileptic condition that grew more severe as she aged and eventually the Balascos, unable to accommodate her at home, placed her in a state mental health facility.

Around the same period that Gail left the household, Mrs. Balasco gave birth to the couple's first child, a daughter, Christine. Figure 3 is a genogram of the current Balasco family.

In retrospect, Mrs. Balasco states that having Christine was a tremendous help to her during a very difficult time that was to occur roughly six months after Christine was born. At that time, within the span of a week, the Balasco family sustained two losses. The first was Mr. Balasco's mother, age 68, who died of "dropsy" after many years of deteriorating health. Mr. Balasco was unable to recall his feelings at the time stating, "It seemed like I went into a web." He remembers trying to forget his mother's death by taking on additional employment. A week after this death, Mrs. Balasco's father died after a long-standing bout with stomach cancer. He had been living with the Balascos for a short time prior to his death and Mrs. Balasco remembers feeling "a great loss, because my father and I were very very close after my mother died."

During the years that followed, Mrs. Balasco remembers "being contented" with her daughter and her home, while Mr. Balasco marks the period by the numerous jobs which he held. Both the Balascos wanted to increase the size of their family. Approximately three and five years after Christine's birth, Mrs. Balasco became pregnant, but miscarried. During this time, she was hospitalized on numerous occasions for D&C procedures and at one point hospital tests revealed that Mrs. Balasco suffered from pernicious anemia, the blood disorder that had proved fatal for her mother (during the years following her mother's death, new approaches to the treatment of pernicious anemia have rendered it non-life-threatening). A little less than a year after her second miscarriage, Mrs. Balasco became pregnant with Teddy and carried him full term. After the delivery, a hysterectomy was suggested due to Mrs. Balasco's ailing health. The Balascos disagreed on this course of action. Mr. Balasco admits that he worried about his wife's health. Mrs. Balasco is unclear about her reasons for not following medical advice at that time. She speculates both that she didn't really understand the gravity of her physical condition and says further, "I had had a lot of sadness in my life and perhaps that was one of the reasons that I kept holding back." Nine months later Mrs. Balasco became pregnant with Davy. The pregnancy was not planned;

Figure 3. Genogram: Current Balasco Family. Darkened square indicates David's position in the family.

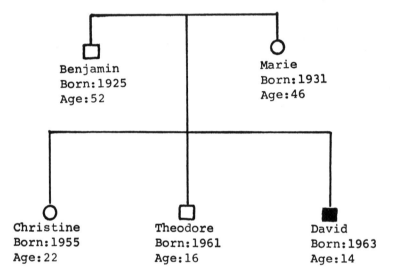

however, the Balascos had taken no precautions to prevent it. The pregnancy was full term and the delivery normal. Five years later, Mrs. Balasco finally consented to a hysterectomy.

Shortly after Davy's birth, Mr. Balasco's father died of a heart attack following a brief illness. Mr. Balasco recalls having a great deal of difficulty accepting his death because "he instilled in us that he was like a god that would never go down." Mr. Balasco admits that he dealt with the death by keeping his feelings to himself and by keeping "both feet rolling." The impact of this death on Mrs. Balasco and Christine and Teddy was minimal as the two children were relatively young at the time and Mrs. Balasco states that she did not know her father-in-law well.

When Davy was a little over a year old, Mrs. Balasco noticed that he had some difficulty walking and a medical examination revealed a crippling disease of the femur joint that necessitated Davy wearing a cast from his thighs down in both legs for four and one-half years and, then, wearing a brace until approximately eight years of age. Both parents agree that Davy's handicap fostered a great deal of closeness and dependence between mother and son. Mr. Balasco admits that he realized that Davy was a "sick kid" and thus didn't make demands on him, but rather turned to and depended on Teddy. Mr. Balasco commented, "You know when your hand is bad you use this hand." Mr. and Mrs. Balasco concur that while Christine and Teddy led fairly normal lives as children, Davy "missed out on a lot." They remember that even when Davy was able to walk unaided, and thus able to begin leading a normal life, that he was quiet and that he did not, like his brother, aggressively seek out friends. During the years that Davy was handicapped, Mrs. Balasco was also ill and frequently hospitalized with complications stemming from her blood condition. During these periods, Christine would assume her mother's responsibilities in the house, including the special care of Davy. At present, only Mr. Balasco and Christine are cognizant of the seriousness of Mrs. Balasco's pernicious anemia. Mrs. Balasco chose to tell her sons that her blood disease was of a less serious nature to avoid worrying them.

In 1972, when Teddy was 11 and Davy 9, Christine graduated from high school and decided to marry. Both Mr. and Mrs. Balasco state that they approved of the marriage although they wish she had waited longer before taking the step. Davy recalls contrary feelings in his family, stating that Christine eloped with her boyfriend during a family vacation because, otherwise, the Balascos would not have permitted the marriage. Mr. and Mrs. Balasco agree that, after the marriage, life seemed pretty much the same as the newlyweds "were living about two streets away." The Balascos state that little changed in the household after Christine left with the exception that the boys each had their own room and became, according to their parents more "independent," where they had previously relied on their sister for numerous things.

In the following years, the Balasco family sustained two losses, both on Mr. Balasco's side of the family. Within two years, Mr. Balasco's oldest brother,

Robert, died of complications resulting from a chronic alcohol condition. Mr. Balasco, referring to his brother as "an odd duck," states that no one in the family was particularly close to him and that his death left little or no impression. However, the death of Mr. Balasco's sister, Lydia, of leukemia, approximately seven months prior to this investigation, had quite an impact on the family and on Davy in particular who recalls, "I loved her so much . . . I would have given up my life so she could have lived."

Shortly after this death, Mr. Balasco was offered a better job in a community roughly an hour from the family home. Because accepting the job involved a long commute, a move was suggested. The entire family agreed that initially they were excited about this possibility but as the time for the move grew closer, the enthusiasm of the two boys decreased significantly and the move became an issue of conflict within the family. This seemed to be a particularly difficult time for Davy who had just begun high school and after many years of being a loner had finally found acceptance from a peer group. However, the Balascos disapproved of these friends and discouraged Davy's contact with them. Davy recalls, "I just finally make friends and then you guys say they're the wrong kind of friends." The struggle over friends became superimposed over the struggle to move and the move began to be perceived by Davy as an intentional plan to disrupt his peer relations. The Balascos date their concern over Davy's emotional stability to an incident that occurred about a month after school began and roughly three months before the family move. Without informing his parents, Davy drove the family car to a neighboring state and back, an action that drew mixed reactions from the Balascos. While Mrs. Balasco was quite worried and upset, Mr. Balasco recollects, "I didn't know that he could drive" and states that he felt "proud and happy" about the episode. Shortly thereafter, Mrs. Balasco found a note of a suicidal nature under the mattress in Davy's room. Concerned over the seriousness of Davy's behavior and the note, Mrs. Balasco took him to a local mental health facility where the intake worker suggested hospitalization for Davy in a psychiatric hospital approximately an hour from the Balasco home. Questioning the need for Davy's hospitalization, the Balascos discussed it with their pediatrician who made a referral to a second mental health facility where a psychiatric evaluation was begun in mid-November of 1976. During the initial phases of the evaluation, Mrs. Balasco found a second suicide note, but states that she told no one and did nothing about it. Psychotherapy for the Balascos commenced in mid-December. In early January, just after the family had moved into their new home, Mrs. Balasco found a third note and informed Davy's therapist, who subsequently evaluated Davy. On the basis of depression and suicidal ideation, the therapist decided to hospitalize him. Davy states that he never knew that his mother had found the suicide notes; in his mind, contact with the mental health facility had been initiated because of his problematic behavior.

Davy was hospitalized for a period of three weeks. After his discharge, both individual and family therapy were continued with the major focus being to help Mrs. Balasco become less involved with her son and to encourage Mr. Balasco to become more involved. After approximately two months of post-hospitalization treatment, Davy initiated a termination with his therapist. The Balascos did not protest this course of action and the entire family ended their contact with the mental health facility at that time.

Interview Impressions

All four of the interview sessions with the Balasco family took place in their home. The interview with Davy was conducted in his bedroom at his request. The remaining three interviews were held around the kitchen table. Three of the meetings were scheduled on weekend days and, typically, when the author arrived at the Balasco home, Mr. Balasco would be hard at work outdoors landscaping the yard, frequently accompanied by his son Teddy. Mrs. Balasco was always inside the house either cleaning or cooking. With the exception of the time that Davy was interviewed, he was not at home during the visits. On the occasion of the last interview, the Balascos were extremely worried because Davy had not been home for two days and they had no idea as to his whereabouts.

Mrs. Balasco is a calm, soft spoken woman with a nonetheless firm manner. Her slightly graying, brown hair makes her appear older than her stated age. During the interview sessions, she was open, cooperative, and seemed quite eager to share thoughts and feelings, particularly about past events in her life. Mrs. Balasco was willing to directly confront painful subject matter even though she proved extremely vulnerable emotionally—frequently crying for long periods of time on these occasions—but insisting that the interview continue. Although the material was disturbing to her, Mrs. Balasco appeared surprisingly at home with her memories of the past, and she conveyed the feeling that she was reliving them as she spoke. At the conclusion of the inquiry with the Balasco family, Mrs. Balasco, without prompting, brought out pictures of members of her family of origin, many of whom had been dead for several years.

In contrast, Mr. Balasco, a dark, handsome man with sharp features, related his narrative in an often abrupt and rhetorical fashion, using intense eye contact and frequently shaking his finger in the air or banging his fist on the table. In particular, when recounting past events, he assumed a dramatic manner which lent a story-telling quality to his recollection of memories. Although generally serious, Mr. Balasco would occasionally punctuate the interview with what might best be described as gruff wit. Most notable was Mr. Balasco's tendency to perseverate on particular themes (i.e., themes involving his strict upbringing or his shortcomings in raising his own children) following the discussion of anxiety-provoking or emotionally-laden topics.

As a couple, the Balasco participated equally in their joint interview sessions. However, at times, the verbal exchange had more the quality of alternating monologues than of mutual interaction. When discussing conflictual topics, particularly issues involving Davy, the inability of the Balascos to acknowledge and assimilate their respective differences of opinion was noteworthy. At these moments, it appeared as if they simply were not listening to one another. Also of note was Mr. Balasco's deference to his wife on factual questions involving potentially emotional topics. For example, when asked when certain members of his family had died, Mr. Balasco turned expectantly to his wife for the specific data. On these occasions she always responded with assurance and accuracy.

The oldest son, Teddy, was present only for a small portion of the family interview. He is a tall, dark, muscular youngster who seemed aloof and angry during his involvement in the session. Although Teddy had read and signed a consent form explaining the nature of the study, he expressed surprise when the interview began, at first stating that he never knew that his brother had written suicide notes; then later amending this statement, explaining that he had learned of the notes from a neighbor. Approximately 15 minutes into the family interview, Teddy abruptly left the kitchen table, seemingly angry that his family had kept the information about Davy's suicide notes from him. Mrs. Balasco made a half-hearted attempt, which met with little success, to reinvolve Teddy in the interview.

Davy, a slight, dark, almost delicate-looking boy, was quiet for much of the family interview; when he did make a contribution, it was done impulsively or, paradoxically, as if he were weighing his words very carefully. Although he was much more verbal and outgoing when interviewed alone, he still seemed conscious of making a good impression and at one point asked, "Am I doing it right?" When asked to describe himself, Davy responded in either a global or surprisingly concrete manner. For instance, in reference to himself he commented, "I got my faults and I got my good points . . . I'm ok." But when asked specifically to elaborate on his "weak points," he explained that he was "not as strong physically" as he "ought to be." With regard to his perceptions of other family members, Davy characterized his mother as "domineering" and "trying to run my life." He perceived his father as "trying to understand everyone's problems and to get everyone together." "Teddy," Davy explained in an almost parental tone, "is flunking . . . that kid is all screwed up." Finally, Davy spoke of his sister Christine as a "good person" and "somebody that I can talk to when she's around."

The Petite Family

Identifying Data

The Petites are a working class Catholic family who reside in a large New England town. In 1967, the Petite family experienced a major change in their socio-economic status when Mr. Petite proved unable to maintain what had been the family's characteristic standard of living. Since that time, the family had moved several times; however, they have always relocated within the same community.

Frederick Petite, age 45, is employed full time by a local caterer. Rose Petite, age 43, holds a part-time job. There are five children in the family. Figure 4 is a genogram of the current Petite family. The oldest children, Kenny, age 25, and Peter, age 22, reside nearby and have been married for three years and two months, respectively. Linda, age 19, lives at home and works in an assembly line at an electronics corporation. Charles, age 16, and Kathy, age 12, both live in the Petite home and attend public school.

Numerous members of the extended families of both Mr. and Mrs. Petite live in adjacent communities. Mrs. Petite's parents are deceased. Mr. Petite's parents reside closeby.

The Petite's middle child, Linda, made two suicide attempts during her sophomore year in high school when she was 16 years old. She was living at home at the time. Three years later, she sought help at a local mental health facility for recurrent depressions. It was through the author's contact with this facility that Linda became involved in the inquiry.

Available Parental History

Both Mr. and Mrs. Petite are of French Canadian descent and were born in New England. Mr. Petite is the youngest child and only son in a family of four children. His oldest sister, Mary, age 50, is married and has one child. Mr. Petite's other two sisters, Simone, age 49, and Catherine, age 47, are presently separated from their respective husbands. Each has five children.

Mrs. Petite was born the last of four daughters. When she was 10 years old, her oldest sister, Loretta, then age 19, died from a malignant brain tumor. Linda remarks that her mother experienced this as a particularly personal loss as of all her sisters, she felt closest to and most involved with Loretta. Although she could not be specific, Linda recalls that within the last 10 years both of her mother's surviving sisters, Madilyn, age 49, and Brigitte, age 45, "had cancer and were cured." Both Madilyn and Brigitte are married and live in the area. They have families of two and five children, respectively. In 1962, Mrs. Petite's mother died of a malignant brain tumor, and in 1967, after a long illness, her father died also from cancer of the brain.

Current Family History: The Adolescent's Perspective

Linda was born in 1958 in the community in which she presently lives. From early on, she remembers feelings of intense loneliness and inadequacy as a child. She recalls that she has never felt that she "belonged" or "fit in" with people outside her family. She admits that frequently she experienced similar feelings in relation to her family itself. These general sentiments are reflected in Linda's earliest

Figure 4.   Genogram: The Petite Family. Darkened circle indicates Linda's position in the family.

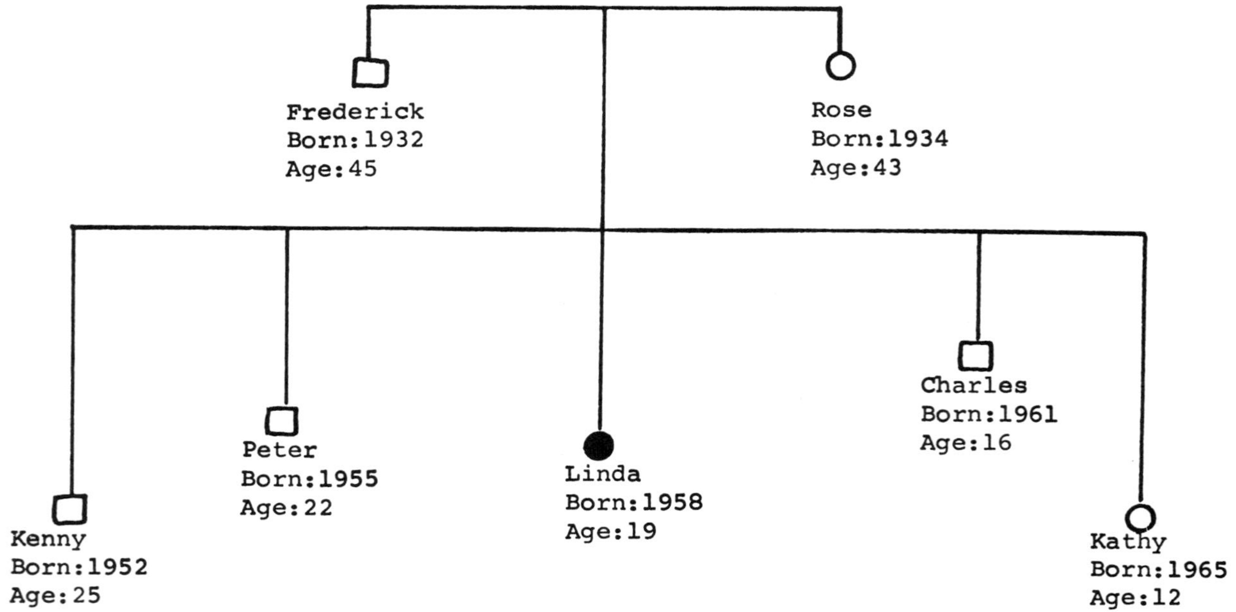

memories of kindergarten. In one memory, she recalls being stranded outside the school building while the other children were inside; in a second memory, she recollects being "looked at funny by the teacher and laughed at by the kids" for doing a paper incorrectly. With regard to her family, she remembers her oldest brother, Kenny, as the special, popular, outgoing child, while she and her brother Peter were "slow," less fortunate, and "outsiders." Linda recollects that as children, she and Peter were constantly being "beaten up" by the other children and that school "was always a problem because the teachers and students made it hard."

Before she had reached the age of 10, Linda experienced two family deaths. Both of her mother's parents died approximately five years apart from malignant brain tumors. Although she was not emotionally close to either grandparent, she remembers wishing that she had known them better. Linda explains that cancer is a sensitive issue for the Petite family because of its high rate of occurrence in Mrs. Petite's family of origin. Mrs. Petite is the only member of her family who has not had cancer, and Linda admits that the possibility of her mother contracting the disease has been a long-time worry in the immediate family. While growing up, Linda recalls that she would often get very "frightened" when her mother took ill and was "lying around." Frequently, during those periods, Linda would "visualize" her mother "as being dead." Linda states that a great deal of her fear stems from the fact that "if something happened to my mother, I would have a lot of responsibilities and I wouldn't be able to do things." Linda admits that she is often afraid that she too will contract cancer, although she observes that other family members do not share this fear for themselves.

A year after the death of her maternal grandfather, the family experienced a downward shift in their socio-economic status. At the time, the family relocated and Mrs. Petite sought and secured a part-time job. Two years later, at age 12, Linda began working to help the family financially. In early adolescence, she was given a job as a housekeeper by an old couple who lived in her neighborhood. During the course of her employment with them, both members of the couple died and Linda recalls their respective deaths as significant and painful losses for her. Throughout adolescence, Linda continued to work at various jobs.

Linda remembers high school as a difficult time during which she felt particularly lonely and cut off from peers. She made her first suicide attempt at the age of 16 in the course of her sophomore year because her boyfriend "took off without saying good-bye" and her family "wouldn't let me do things." She states that both parents spoke with her after the attempt and she specifically recalls her father saying that "he loved me and he didn't want me to go." Less than a year later, during a period of intense loneliness, Linda made a second suicide attempt by cutting her wrist.

After graduating high school at age 18, Linda initiated two major changes in her life. She abandoned the Catholic faith to become involved in the Reborn

Christian movement, and she left the Petite home to room with two other girls in a nearby apartment. She claims that both actions were extremely difficult for her parents to accept. In retrospect, she feels that of all the children, her leavetaking demanded the most adjustment from her parents. Seven months later, Linda moved back into the family home partly because of financial problems and partly because "there was a strong pull to return home." She explains that she came home again mainly to make her mother happy.

Interview Impressions

Linda is a brown-haired, slender adolescent of average height. She presented as casually but carefully dressed and neatly groomed. When given the choice, Linda decided to complete the inquiry in one extended interview session which took place at the mental health facility where she was in psychotherapy. During the interview, she proved quite articulate and capable of a surprisingly sophisticated level of conceptualization regarding her history and current problems. At times, her affect seemed flat; however, she did express a great deal of sadness when remembering certain events, and at one point, became so tearful that the interview was temporarily interrupted.

During the interview, Linda described herself in the following way:

> I don't think that I'm a bad person . . . I've got faults, but I think that I'm a good person . . . have a good heart . . . I hate when I get angry . . . when somebody needs something, I would give it to them. I like things that aren't materialistic . . . I'm very sensitive . . . I don't feel that I'm very smart as far as knowledge like science or math, but I feel smart when it comes to feelings.

Linda also characterized her mother as a "very sensitive" person but complained that she is too much of an "authority" and not enough of a "friend." Mr. Petite was described as "kind of stubborn and prejudiced" because "his parents were from the old school." However, Linda also acknowledged her father's kind and loving qualities and, at one point, she cried while recounting her understanding of his feelings for her. Kenny, the oldest boy, was always envisioned by Linda as "being born under a lucky star" because "he always got what he wanted" materially while growing up. She described him as engaging, sociable, and "fitting in" wherever he happens to be. Linda is strongly identified with her other brother, Peter, primarily because both were "outsiders" as children. Linda explained that Peter is a little slow at learning things, but that once "he learns something, he's good at it." Linda spoke of her younger brother, Charles, as "making friends easily" and being "really active in school." The youngest child, Kathy, was described simply as "good" but "very young" for her age and "not interested in boys." When discussing her sister, Linda included Kathy's budding interest in cheerleading and her popularity with peers. With the exception of Peter, Linda stated that she feels different from all her siblings because "they always got involved in things which I never did."

The Franklin Family

Identifying Data

The Franklins are a working class family who reside in a moderate size New England town. The family has lived in their current home for the past 15 years.

George Franklin, age 46, has been employed steadily as a packer for a local company since the birth of the children. Joan Franklin, age 42, began working part-time five years ago to supplement the family income. There are five children in the Franklin family. Figure 5 is a genogram of the current Franklin family. The oldest child, Carlene, age 21, holds a full time job and lives at home. Nancy, age 19, is employed at a local nursing home, and six months prior to the inquiry had moved out of the family house into a two-room apartment in the area. The three boys, Steve, age 18, Stuart, age 13, and David, age 11, all reside at home. The two younger boys attend public school.

Numerous members of the extended family live in the general area. Mr. Franklin's mother is deceased.

The second oldest child, Nancy, has a history of several suicide attempts. She made four attempts on her life during the year prior to the inquiry. All the attempts occurred while she was living at home. For the past several years, Nancy has been attending counseling at a local drop-in center for troubled adolescents. It was through this agency that she came to the author's attention.

Available Parental History

Nancy volunteered little history about her parents. Mr. Franklin is a native of the area and is one of many sisters and brothers. Prior to his only marriage to Nancy's mother, he spent many years in the Navy. In 1976, Mr. Franklin lost his mother who died of brain cancer after a prolonged illness. Nancy states that her father was very close to his mother and was saddened greatly by her death. Mr. Franklin's father is still alive and resides nearby.

Mrs. Franklin is the oldest of three children. She has a younger sister and brother. Mrs. Franklin's sister, Elaine, 18 years her junior, made a suicide attempt seven years ago while residing with the Franklin family. The reason for the attempt is unclear. After the attempt, Nancy recalls that "they wouldn't let Elaine come back to the house . . . they put her away somewhere."

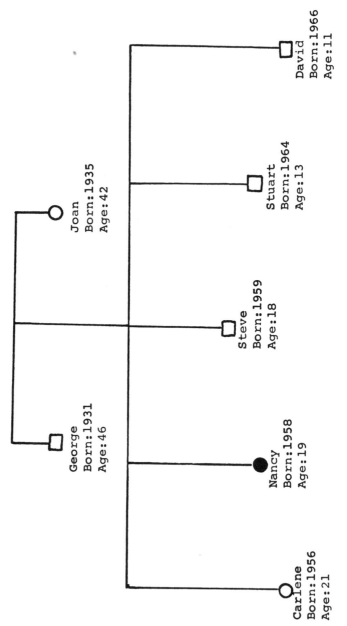

Figure 5. Genogram: The Franklin Family. Darkened circle indicates Nancy's position in the family.

Current Family History: The Adolescent's Perspective

Nancy was born in 1958, the second child and daughter in the Franklin family. From her earliest years, through and after the arrival of her three brothers, Nancy remembers feeling like a loner and a peripheral family member. She vividly recalls both parents threatening from time to time that she was not their child. Consequently, she harbors the fantasy that she's adopted. In addition, she recollects a family life in which everyone, including her parents, was constantly fighting. Of her parents she remarks, "It's like my mother being a cat and my father a dog." Nancy also remembers her mother frequently telling her father in the midst of a fight to "get out." Nancy asserts, "It didn't bother me because it would just mean getting rid of one more undesirable person." Nancy recalls being constantly picked on in the family "because I was the dumb one." Her experiences at home were recapitulated in school. When she was in the third grade, school personnel discovered that Nancy had a hearing problem and consequently she was placed in a special class with other "slow children." She recollects people making fun of her academic status and states, "even my mother would call me 'retarded.'" She cites this negative feedback as the reason behind her decision to skip school classes in the following years.

Nancy admits that all her life she has had thoughts of killing herself or killing others and, in fact, made her first suicide attempt at the age of 10, when, after a fight with her mother about school, she tried to hang herself from the stair railing. At 13, she entertained thoughts of killing her mother and father, and actually tried to stab her sister after a fight but was stopped by a babysitter. It was around this time that Nancy's mother began to drink heavily and became "an alcoholic." Shortly after, Nancy began to skip school and take drugs. She remembers frequently feeling depressed and turning to drugs for an escape. Her friends, she feels, were never available "to hear about it" when she was depressed. During this period, Nancy had an accident in which she fell down some stairs and sustained an arm injury which eventually required hospitalization. She recalls being frightened in the hospital when "they had me strapped down to the table and they took a white sheet and put it over my head like this person is dead." Nancy also angrily remembers receiving no visits from her family during the hospitalization.

The next several years were unhappy ones for Nancy and she has trouble recalling them accurately. It was a period during which she ran away from home several times because she was having problems at school and at home and thought her family would be "happier" without her. She states, though, that her father always came after her and reasons that it was "because he needed somebody to give hell to . . . he wanted somebody to beat up." In her seventeenth year, Nancy became pregnant twice and decided to have an abortion each time because she was afraid of delivering a deformed child as a result of her drug history. In addition, she asserts "if my parents found out, my father would have told me to get out and never come back." Nancy states that she feels very guilty about the abortions and expresses concern that she will someday be punished by God for her behavior. When she was 18 and still in high school, Nancy was "thrown out of the house" for quitting her part-time job. However, school personnel negotiated her reentry into the home. During the same year, she experienced her first death in the family. Her paternal grandmother died after a prolonged illness. Nancy recalls her parents forcing her to go to the wake even though she didn't want to attend because "I'm afraid of dead people."

It was against the backdrop of these events of her late adolescent years that Nancy made four attempts to take her life. She cites as reasons for the attempts, trouble in school and with her family, and just being "sick of everything." Notably two of her attempts followed her first abortion. Although vague about her parent's reaction to three of her attempts, she vividly remembers her father's reaction to a fourth. She recollects her father "putting up his fist and threatening to beat me up." At the beginning of her nineteenth year, Nancy moved out of her house permanently. She remembers that she was the first of the children to do so. Nancy commented that unlike previous occasions, her parents had almost no reaction to her decision to leave.

Interview Impressions

Nancy participated in two interview sessions, both of which took place at the adolescent drop-in center where she was involved in counseling. She was 15 or 30 minutes early for each session and was cooperative but tense throughout. Nancy is a short, plump teenager with freckles and light brown frizzy hair, who was attired for both sessions in boots, dungarees, a sweater, and an army fatigue jacket. Throughout the interviews, Nancy's manner alternated between a casual toughness and a childlike naiveté. When discussing life events, her affect was generally appropriate.

Nancy described herself as an individual who likes people and tries to be honest with them. She did comment though that, "I'll take so much from somebody and then I'll start to fight back." Nancy felt that involvement with drugs is her weak point and she stated that she's always running: "I try to run away from things hoping they'll clear up."

Nancy's description of family members reflected her feeling of alienation from all but her youngest brother, David. She described her father as an angry man who "can't sit down and have a simple conversation with you; he always yells." Nancy referred to her mother as "an alcoholic," who's "a bitch when she's drunk. . . you can't even say boo to her." Carlene, the oldest in the family, was characterized as someone who "flares up a lot." Nancy spoke of her brothers as always fighting among themselves or with her or her parents. The one exception was her brother David who she recalled used to "stick up" for her when she was in trouble. Overall, Nancy described a family in which relationships are characterized by hostility and lack of communication.

4

Loss and Separation: Associated Affects and Cognitions

All events within, as well as outside, the family sphere have affective and cognitive associations for family members. Loss and separation are predictable occurrences within life, and have associated meanings and feelings for members of a given family. These meanings and affects, in addition to the occurrence of the events themselves, will ultimately determine the role that loss and separation will play *vis à vis* a family system. One approach to understanding thoughts and feelings about loss and separation in a family is to explore through history these events and the circumstances surrounding them with family members. The purely historical information presented here, however, need not be taken as accurate; its accuracy is not where its importance lies. Rather, it is significant in reflecting the emotional and cognitive themes that are foreground for those involved in the remembering process. Kantor (1975) notes that "many historic themes are based on events which either did not take place at all or were radically different from the way in which they are remembered." He further states that what is important about historic themes, "is not that they resurrect past events as they actually happened, but that the content and processes associated with such themes recur in the present." Thus, an exploration of events in the remote and recent past, as well as the present, may yield cognitive and affective themes about loss and separation which have roots several generations back.

A basic assumption of the study was that the meaning of loss and separation would prove important in families with a suicidal adolescent member. The data gathered from the members of the Balasco family, as well as the adolescent participants, provides numerous examples of cognitive and affective themes involving loss and separation. These themes are reflected not only in the content of the narrative but also in the manner in which family members, individually and together, convey information. Examples drawn from the narrative of the Balasco family are particularly illustrative of the historical quality of such themes. These data are rich with information about loss and separation which spans three generations; consequently, it illuminates the transmission of cognitive and affective thematic material across generational boundaries.

Family Findings

Family of Origin: Mrs. Balasco

The first memory of note, drawn from Mrs. Balasco's family of origin, concerns her birth which occurred prematurely, shortly after the oldest boy in the family was killed in an accident. Mrs. Balasco recalls:

> He was killed by a truck. It came up on the sidewalk and killed him. So I only weighed two pounds when I was born. Apparently, when this happened to my brother, it was almost a still-birth type of thing. My mother must have gone through some kind of emotional strain. I know from my aunts talking that I lived for two months in the hospital because my digestive system was really bad. I guess I couldn't keep anything in my stomach. So I was quite a few months in the hospital before I was home. And then, I came home but apparently, I had gone back into the hospital for some time again and I've always had a problem with my stomach.

Here a birth is associated with a death. The loss of the oldest child has such a powerful effect that a second child is almost lost. As Mrs. Balasco reconstructs her birth and the first few months of life, a picture of physical fragility and tenuous survival emerges. She connects progressively the loss of her brother to the health problems suffered throughout her life. Thus, she suggests that loss represents not only a threat to her survival at birth, but a threat to her on-going physical well-being as well. Mrs. Balasco intimates that she is never entirely free from the impact caused by the original loss. The following dialogue with Mrs. Balasco further illustrates beliefs which she holds about the relation of her own development to the family's loss of the oldest son. The focus of the interchange is Mrs. Balasco's sister, Evelyn, who was unable to talk.

Mrs. Balasco: Now I only know this through my aunt . . . I don't know why, but we would kind of lead her and she would make sounds and apparently we used to do the same thing; that's why sometimes I tend to wonder whether my brother being killed had an effect on my mother. I think that in some ways it must have, but you know, you just hate to say things like that.

Interviewer: What do you mean?

Mrs. Balasco: Because apparently my brother and I were certainly healthy as far as normal intelligence goes, even my brother, Jimmy, and yet we really didn't talk, we just made sounds too.

Interviewer: So you're wondering why your mother didn't intervene and get you talking?

Mrs. Balasco: Yes.

With these thoughts, Mrs. Balasco expresses an aunt's, as well as her own, fantasy that her brother's death proved so emotionally debilitating for her mother that she was unable to help her children through a crucial developmental stage. A third recollection underscores the disabling aspects of loss. In reference to the dead child, Alan, and the two handicapped children, Evelyn and Jimmy, Mrs. Balasco speculates:

> I would think . . . my mother dying at that young age, plus she had a blood condition, those three children, that burden was just too much for her . . . because all of her sisters and brothers lived to be good ages. No, I think that it was too hard for her to cope with her first three, I'm sure it did a job on her.

Here, Mrs. Balasco associates loss with deteriorating health and eventual death. The link between poor health and loss is present again in Mrs. Balasco's description of the onset of her ulcer disease just a few months after the death of her mother.

When asked how she and other family members experienced their mother's death, Mrs. Balasco struggles to put her thoughts together and in the process openly grapples with the meaning of the event. She states tearfully:

> At the time, I don't know . . . when I think back on it when my father come home and said that my mother had died . . . my mother was only in the hospital for two days . . you know that we didn't realize that my mother was that sick . . . we didn't know anybody that went to the hospital and I didn't know what it means when somebody dies. Well I guess you do know what it means when somebody dies, but really you don't know what it means either. But when my father come home and said, "Get the kids cleaned up," I did.

In this statement, Mrs. Balasco speaks of the circumstances surrounding her mother's death in an almost apologetic tone, referring to her own and her family's feelings of ignorance regarding the loss. There seems to be an association between loss and a deficiency in the cognitive realm. Mrs. Balasco emphasizes her inability to conceptualize loss at the time; and with a shift in tense stresses her inability to comprehend loss in the present as well. However, her concluding comment reflects an attribution of meaning. She recalls her father's demand that she "get the kids cleaned up," making an association between loss and unmet needs. When her mother dies, her father and the rest of the family become dependent on her and she states, "That's the way it was after that." Thus, her association of loss and dependency is made not only to a particular event or moment in time but also to an ongoing period in the life of the family. In Mrs. Balasco's memory, the absence of her mother marks the beginning of the family's explicit dependence on her.

When discussing her mother's death, Mrs. Balasco displayed a considerable amount of sad affect. She began to cry openly shortly after the topic was raised and she cried sporadically for the duration of that particular interview. During the discussion, Mrs. Balasco frequently punctuated her affect with statements like:

> I'm sorry I don't usually talk about it because I know that this happens. I probably need some help myself.

> Oh, I just can't think about it, I don't know why it still bothers me. I never can talk about it. You'd think after 30 years it wouldn't bother me no more.

> I guess I've always thought that when you lose your parents you don't cry enough. When you're older and you lose someone you really get it out of your system, but when you're young it doesn't register . . . at least until you cry enough, it's just there.

With these comments, Mrs. Balasco links childhood loss to feelings that are powerful and enduring. Again her remarks assume an apologetic quality and convey a sense of personal inadequacy, this time in the emotional realm. She seems to feel helpless and deficient in the face of the potent affect evoked by remembered loss; she subsequently expresses reluctance even to think or talk about it, lest she be overwhelmed by feelings.

When asked, Mrs. Balasco is unable to recall how the rest of her family felt about her mother's death when it occurred, and she insists that even now, 30 years later, she is unaware of their reactions. She comments, "They may feel the same way that I do, I don't know." While she is able to share the affect associated with her mother's death in the interview, she admits that she never broaches the subject with members of her family of origin because:

> I really don't know if they can talk about it. I don't talk about it to them because I know that I always cry. If I tried to talk about it, I'll end up like this.

Mrs. Balasco's reluctance to discuss the loss with members of her family under-scores her associated feelings of emotional inadequacy. She wonders if her family, like herself, will prove unable to talk about and bear the feelings raised by loss.

Briefly, to summarize, Mrs. Balasco's associations to events of loss and separation in her family of origin fall into a number of thematic categories. A major theme surfaces in Mrs. Balasco's repeated linking of physical disability and illness with loss. A second theme relates to Mrs. Balasco's associations to loss as an unthinkable, unspeakable, and emotionally unmanageable event. These associa-tions are mediated by the theme of personal deficiency in the affective and cognitive realms. Dependency, an association which Mrs. Balasco makes not only to an event of loss, but also to a period of time following that event, emerges as a third salient theme.

Family of Origin: Mr. Balasco

Mr. Balasco's recollections of loss and separation in his family of origin present some thematic complements as well as contrasts to the memories of his wife. Overall, Mr. Balasco's narrative conveys a picture of a strict, task-oriented family life on a farm where the children "were brought up as a working machine." The farm was the family's sole source of livelihood and its survival literally depended on the crops and animals raised on the land. The rate of production corresponded to the number of Balasco children in residence on the farm. When the children grew older and started to leave home, Mr. Balasco recalls:

> Then for my father the reality came, the workhorses had left. The production of the farm fell apart . . . wagons that were supposed to be moved everyday were moved once a month.

After several years in the Navy, Mr. Balasco returned home to find only his parents, his youngest sister, Theresa, and his handicapped brother, Peter. In this recollection he presents an image of stagnation:

> The farm had dwindled . . . the cows had gone to nothing. In some of the years I don't think some of the stuff had moved in 10 or 12 years. Pieces of equipment were all in the fields.

Thinking back to the years just prior to his second marriage, Mr. Balasco admits:

> The farm had really closed down because when the labor takes off . . . and they had no money to pay.

In these and many other similar statements, Mr. Balasco associates deterioration and disruption of productive forces on the farm with the departure of the Balasco children. Here, the gradual loss of the children or "the working machine" presents a progressively serious threat to the family's survival.

Mr. Balasco comments on the termination of his first marriage in a similar vein:

> Well I got married to a neighborhood girl. Within a year and a half I was separated and five years later I was divorced, but more or less I think that the farm was the cause of it because we couldn't make a living at it.

> I can never knock that girl. Even today I think to myself, if only we had had a week's pay we would have been together.

With these comments, Mr. Balasco associates a major separation in his life with the inability to produce on the farm.

Paradoxically, abundant production on the farm also carried negative associations for Mr. Balasco. Living on a farm sensitized him to repeated loss and separation because of the perpetual harvesting of crops and slaughter of animals. He recollects becoming "despondent at killing time." He explains:

> Once you've been a farmer, anything tied to the land, death is a very bad thing . . . I never liked to see things die, even when the corn was cut and being blown into the silo, the corn was so high and then we would have to cut it and blow it in and it was kind of sad seeing this thing produce so well that you had to kill it. I may not show it but I'm not partial to busting up things.

Mr. Balasco recollects these feelings about the slaughter of animals:

> I had a hard time with animals on the farm at killing time. We . . . I used to get very despondent because my father would cut out of the herd of 4-500 about 20 to 30 pigs to be slaughtered. I used to feel pretty bad. These were animals that you saw born from a litter and that you took care of and this kind of bothered me, but what could I do?

Although harvest and slaughter helped the family survive, Mr. Balasco had difficulty accepting the loss involved, and he recalls feelings of disruption, hopelessness, sadness, and helplessness in conjunction with abundant farm production. Most notably, he links growth with loss, and association which is congruent with an earlier link between the departure of the Balasco children and the deterioration of the farm. As the children grew and left home, the farm became barren, and as a result, the remaining members of the Balasco family could barely survive.

The following dialogue between Mr. Balasco and the investigator about the two children who preceded him in the birth order and died of black diphtheria reveals further associations to loss.

Interviewer: Did your family ever talk about the two children before you that died when they were infants?

Mr. Balasco: Yes, there was talk, that I was next, that they thought that I was going.

Interviewer: They were one and two years old when they died and you were an infant?

Mr. Balasco: I wasn't even born.

Interviewer: How was it that they thought that you were going if you weren't born yet?

Mr. Balasco: After I was born I had the same thing and as I recall many of them talking about it they gave me a shot of orange juice and castor oil, but I was turning just like them, blue and everything else and they said that I was going to go but for some ungodly reason I survived.

Interviewer: So, when you were older you heard that they had talked about the fact that they thought that you were next. How did you feel hearing that?

Mr. Balasco: It felt kind of gruesome to a certain degree that I was here and the other ones were gone, but you know never once did I ask if there was any difference between them and me . . . at their age that they passed away.

Interviewer: What do you mean, difference?

Mr. Balasco: If I was any different than them or how I acted or anything like that. I didn't want to be compared. Nobody likes comparisons. As I go through life I always remember this . . . I do not care what anybody else is or what they want to do. I always think that I can count on me and like I said, I'm a loner.

The associative processes which occur in this interchange suggest a strong link between Mr. Balasco and his two dead brothers, or between Mr. Balasco and impending loss ("they said that I was going to go . . . "). Mr. Balasco's unprompted introduction of the topic of comparison underscores the association, and his subsequent associative flight from that subject to self reliance and isolation implies that the link between himself and his dead brothers may be one that is difficult to sustain affectively and cognitively. Indeed, Mr. Balasco's remarks intimate his perception of a merging of early identities; as he recalls it, the family's loss of his brothers seem synonymous with its anticipated loss of him. Thus, in this way, he sees his own survival as tenuous. Mr. Balasco associates vulnerability and helplessness with his own anticipated loss and, paradoxically, morbid feelings about his survival ("it was gruesome . . . ").

Later in the narrative, Mr. Balasco again refers to himself as " a loner," this time when addressing the topic of friends. His remarks illustrate his difficulty sustaining a relationship when the affects and cognitions associated with loss or separation are involved. He states:

> Like I told you, I'm a loner and I had one friend that I met while I was in the linen business and he was my closest friend that I ever had until he separated from his wife. Like I told you before, I just don't want nobody else's problems. If I want to get up from this table and go and lie down and I don't want to have to worry about the guy next door and his problems.

Here, Mr. Balasco sees his friend's marital separation as posing a threat to Mr. Balasco's everyday routine and, thus, as representing a worry and a burden. Mr. Balasco expresses a strong preference not to be involved in these problems. He simply refuses to associate himself with separation, choosing instead isolation from his "closest friend."

In summary, Mr. Balasco's affective and cognitive associations to loss comprise a number of themes. Throughout his narrative, Mr. Balasco consistently associates loss and separation with farm production in both its barren and fertile phases. Thus, a pronounced associative theme for Mr. Balasco involves contrasting aspects of growth. Predominant affective themes include hopelessness and helplessness. Finally, Mr. Balasco's flight from direct personal association with loss and separation suggests that he questions his ability to manage the affects and cognitions involved and experiences them as a threat to daily existence. He seems to turn to isolation from events of loss and separation as a resolution. This pattern of experience and action constitutes a third salient associative theme of inadequacy.

Mr. and Mrs. Balasco's associations to loss and separation in their respective families of origin reveal that they share a number of meanings and affects about these events, although at times the particular themes which unify their associations vary. Both Mr. and Mrs. Balasco associate loss and separation with a threat to family survival; however, the thematic representation of this threat differs for each. For Mrs. Balasco, the associated threat is one of physical debilitation, while for Mr. Balasco, the threat is one of infertility and subsequent unavailability of necessary sustenance. Similarly, the Balascos perceive loss as a threat to their personal survival, as suggested in their individual associations of vulnerability at birth to the death of the children preceding them. The impact of the loss of the earlier children on Mr. and Mrs. Balasco seems to linger for both, although in differing ways. Mrs. Balasco associates her own continued physical fragility with the loss, while Mr. Balasco links his own persistent emotional vulnerability with the early deaths. Within the affective sphere, although each of the Balascos makes a number of idiosyncratic associations to loss and separation, both share feelings of inadequacy in this realm. Mr. and Mrs. Balasco express reluctance to talk or think about loss and separation and both appear to doubt their ability—as well as the ability of others—to manage the particular affects and cognitions associated with loss and separation.

The Current Balasco Family

As the Balascos talk about events of loss and separation spanning the first 10 years of their marriage, familiar associative themes reappear. The most readily recalled losses by both Balascos were the deaths of their parents. Mr. Balasco's mother and Mrs. Balasco's father died within a week of each other, roughly two years into the Balascos' married life. Mr. Balasco's father died approximately four years later. Of note, the interchange between the Balascos about these deaths during the interviews is marked by particular behaviors. Mr. Balasco consistently defers to his wife regarding factual information pertinent to these losses. For example, he asks about the year in which each individual died and the chronological relationship among the deaths. On these occasions, Mrs. Balasco responds quickly in an almost rote manner to provide information. However, once the actual circumstances of the deaths are discussed, Mrs. Balasco begins to weep quietly and continues to cry throughout the discussion. Her display of affect represents a notable contrast to her husband's controlled emotional stance.

When asked about her feelings regarding the closely occurring deaths of her father and mother-in-law, Mrs. Balasco replies:

> I think it made it easier in one way because Christine was a baby. My time was pretty much taken up with her and that probably helped me not to feel quite as badly as I might have if I had not had her.

She was asked to elaborate and she continues:

> Well Christine was a baby and she needed me to be there all the time. Well, I don't know if I put more work into Christine. I'm not sure, I was so thrilled that I had her because all of that time I didn't think I was going to have a child.

Here, Mrs. Balasco responds to a question about loss with an association to a newly born baby whose needs preoccupied her. She concludes that statement by commenting on the strong uncertainty in her mind surrounding the birth of the baby. These associations which Mrs. Balasco makes to loss, bear a strong resemblance to those which she makes earlier to events of loss and separation in her family of origin: birth and death are linked; birth is thought of as tenuous; and the needs of others become predominant. However, the most notable similarity to her earlier associations is illustrated by Mrs. Balasco's presentation of affect around the topic. Although denying that the two deaths had a major impact upon her, Mrs. Balasco cries throughout the discussion and when asked how long it took her to get over the deaths she responds, "I don't think that I could ever forget." Again, both her remarks and her emotional stance suggest that she experiences loss as potent and enduring.

At different points in the narrative, when referring to his mother's death, Mr. Balasco makes the association of loss with deterioration of farm production. He first recollects a period of time after his return from the service when he lived for a while on the declining farm. Finally deciding to end permanently his residence there, he takes a job elsewhere and recalls:

> I used to go back to the farm and help on my days off and cut hay for them . . . but I noticed in my mother that she was failing.

Thus, as he recalls the time period leading up to his mother's death, Mr. Balasco connects her failing health to the deteriorating farm. There is also an implication that he associates personal inadequacy or helplessness with his mother's death as he recollects that despite his efforts to produce (i.e., "cut hay"), his mother's health fails. A second statement made later in the narrative regarding the actual death of his mother again pairs poor farm production and loss. Mr. Balasco recollects:

> She died of dropsy. She had a heart condition. You see the history of my family goes way back, at that particular time, we were having a little trouble with the farm.

The following interchange illuminates other associations made by Mr. Balasco to the loss of his mother.

Interviewer: How long did it take you to forget?

Mr. Balasco: Well it took a good year and a half to two years.

Interviewer: So it took some time to adjust?

Mr. Balasco: I never said much.

Interviewer: You kept things to yourself.

Mr. Balasco: Like I told you, I'm a loner. If I got anything to say like if a guy is going to get me mad then I say it but other than that, I see a lot of things in the world that I would talk about but there's no sense. It doesn't give us any welfare.

With these comments, Mr. Balasco again identifies himself as "a loner" in respect to loss, expressing reluctance to talk about and share this experience; he associates doing so with a threat to his well-being and the well-being of others.

Regarding the death of his father, Mr. Balasco recalls:

That one . . . I never dreamed that this man could have a heart condition because of how strong he was but when I found out that he went to the hospital it really slayed me. He instilled in us that he was like a god that could never go down. When I went to the hospital to see him it kind of hurt me to see him laying down like that. Those are things that I haven't told anybody but that have stayed with me for awhile. I see this powerful person down. I didn't expect to see the things that I saw in him in the last.

Dominant in this statement is an association between loss of power, or helplessness, and loss itself. Foreground in Mr. Balasco's memory are his father's submission to illness and subsequent loss of power as well as Mr. Balasco's own reaction of feeling "slayed" or helpless. Mr. Balasco's words also reflect a strong association of disillusionment and loss. In addition, he alludes to the enduring quality of his reactions and confirms earlier feelings of reluctance to talk with others about his responses and reactions to loss.

In the following interchange Mr. Balasco provides some understanding of the manner in which the respective associative themes to loss made by the Balascos interact withing the marital relationship.

Interviewer: Did you turn to each other during these times for support?

Mr. Balasco: Oh, my wife is very supportful. I used to see her crying over the stove because of her father and I knew that my mother's mixed emotions were involved in it too.

Interviewer: Would you say that your wife was doing the crying for both of you?

Mr. Balasco: I think she was, because she did it all through. Well I think that she has always done it, because I don't show emotion sometimes, maybe I have it inside because I'm human . . . but I try not to fall like a baby. I try to keep my thoughts together as a man.

The lack of reference in these comments to any verbal exchange between the Balascos suggests that they are just as reluctant to discuss loss within the context of their marriage as they are with other individuals. Mr. Balasco's associative juxtaposition of his wife as an emotional sponge and his own fear of falling helplessly ("like a baby") in the face of loss implies a reliance upon his wife to manage the affects associated with loss and separation. Thus, within the marital relationship, Mr. Balasco defers to his wife to handle the feelings connected with loss much in the way that he looks to her to manage the factual or more cognitive aspects of loss as demonstrated earlier. Mr. Balasco's reliance upon his wife in both the cognitive and affective realms is congruent with his isolative stance regarding loss and separation and his associations of helplessness and inadequacy. Thus, Mr.

Balasco feels a need for his wife's emotional management to preclude his becoming helpless and unmanly. This complements a predominant associative theme of Mrs. Balasco's, the creation of needs and dependency in conjunction with loss. Although she perceives herself as inept at the management of the affects and cognitions linked with loss, she seems to accept implicitly her husband's dependency on her within this context. Mr. Balasco, just as he did in earlier recollections, represents himself within the marriage as a loner, disassociating himself from the unmanageable aspects of loss and separation. This disassociation mainly seems to be accomplished through a minimization of loss-related communication with his wife. Mrs. Balasco also represents herself within the context of her marriage as she did in earlier memories, as being strongly gripped by the potent and enduring aspects of loss and separation; although she, like her husband, experiences them as unmanageable. Like her husband, Mrs. Balasco isolates herself by not talking about or sharing feelings about loss and separation. However, while Mr. Balasco's isolation supposedly frees him from experiencing the affects and cognitions associated with loss, Mrs. Balasco's isolation serves to immerse her in the very affects and cognitions that she seems to fear. Within the marriage, as long as talk about loss and separation is minimized, the relative isolation of the Balascos is reinforced and they are free to play out complementary roles in the realm of dependency.

Later in the interview session, when asked to reflect on losses and separations after the birth of the children, Mrs. Balasco introduces the topic of her miscarriages and frequent hospitalizations. As she tries to remember this period of time, she begins to cry and admits:

> It's very hard for me to think back, I've been through a lot of things. I guess I cry without even thinking I'm crying.

Again her associations stress the difficulty of thinking about loss as well as its persistent and potent affective qualities. Tearfully, she describes her second miscarriage, the subsequent births of her last two children, and the consideration of a hysterectomy:

> Christine was about three and one-half and then before I had Teddy I was pregnant four and one-half months and I lost that baby. Now Christine would have been about five at that time . . . but that was a very difficult miscarriage because I had evidently miscarried the baby but I didn't miscarry the placenta and I was very sick at home for a long time not realizing that I was going through labor and at that time finally, I just . . . every time that I got out of bed there was just massive bleeding and finally I said to Ben, "I have to go to the hospital, I have to go somewhere and get some help," and sure enough I had lost the baby and that baby was supposed to be born the September before Teddy was born, so I got pregnant right away after I had that.

When asked how she handled a sudden loss like that, she responds:

Well, I really felt badly because I did want other children and where I had had many problems with my periods and I had had D&Cs and so forth, to try to correct the situation, I just thought perhaps I wouldn't have anymore children so when I got pregnant for Teddy I was more than careful hoping that things would go along fine and fortunately they did go along fine. And then, we discussed my having a hysterectomy at that time after I had had Teddy, and I just really kind of wanted to wait . . . you know I've had a serious blood condition for years. I didn't realize at the time how serious it is . . . and then I got pregnant with Davy and I felt that I shouldn't push my luck any further even though I did want more children, at the time it was just at the point that if I pushed my luck any further, I might not be here to take care of them. So I decided all in all that it was best that it was done . . . it was quite a traumatic thing that I went through and fortunately I'm still here.

These lengthy statements reflect an interplay of associative themes which previously have proven salient for Mrs. Balasco. In response to the loss of an unborn child and the potential loss of her child-bearing capabilities, Mrs. Balasco alludes to birth, the tenuousness of birth, physical fragility, enduring physical illness (i.e., "a serious blood condition"), trauma, and finally the tenuousness of her own survival. The appearance of this configuration of associations in an account of a lost child is notably reminiscent of Mrs. Balasco's earlier associative links to the loss of her brother Alan. In addition, Mrs. Balasco's associative progression from a serious blood condition to the birth of her third child, Davy, to the tenuousness of her own survival, bears a striking resemblance to an earlier association made to her mother's death. Despite the fact that Mrs. Balasco alludes to the conception and birth of both Teddy and Davy in her statement, Davy seem to occupy a special associative position. Although only implied in these statements, Mrs. Balasco explains elsewhere in the narrative the medically documented cause and effect relationship between her blood condition and gynecological problems. The serious nature of her illness made child-bearing increasingly dangerous for her. Thus, as the last child conceived, Davy posed the most serious threat to his mother's health, in addition to being at high risk himself. Notably in her statement, it is her reference to Davy that is associatively bound by comments about the seriousness of her blood condition and the tenuousness of her survival. Mrs. Balasco's associations imply that either Davy or herself, or to a lesser degree Teddy, were potential objects of loss for the family.

Mr. Balasco proved quite subdued during the discussion about his wife's child-bearing difficulties, and when asked about his reaction to the second miscarriage sparingly responds:

Well I was kind of depressed because you know this girl was sick all the time and with Christine around and I was working two jobs, it was quite a strain.

Here, on the topic of the loss of an unborn child and separations from his wife necessitated by her frequent hospitalizations, Mr. Balasco associates to depression and the strain placed on him by the demands made by others, the implied connection to loss and separation being feelings of inadequacy. Regarding the period of time following the birth of Teddy when Mrs. Balasco had been advised to have a hysterectomy, Mr. Balasco recalls:

> I was worried about her . . . and if I was ever left with two little small children and a big house.

The prevailing association here seems to be to the permanent loss of Mrs. Balasco herself. A second implied association is Mr. Balasco's inadequacy in the face of this loss. Mr. Balasco's link of the events of this period of time with the loss of his wife are congruent with her preoccupation of the same events and the tenuousness of her survival. Both Balascos associate to the potential death of Mrs. Balasco directly before and after the birth of their third child, Davy. Davy seems to be both explicitly (for Mrs. Balasco) and implicitly (for Mr. Balasco) associated to the potential loss of Mrs. Balasco. Speculatively, Davy may represent a personification of anticipated loss for the Balascos.

Notably, as the talk about loss and separation in the family after the birth of the children continues, the subject of Davy dominates the discussion even though as a child he was never separated from the family. Mrs. Balasco explains that due to a bone disease, Davy lost the use of his legs for roughly three of his first four years of life and required braces for the following four years. Both parents recall this time as a critical one in their lives, and their associations to Davy's temporary loss of his legs and their own loss of a normal child are congruent with past associative themes. Mrs. Balasco recollects spending "⁹⁄₁₀ths" of her time at home attending to Davy's needs. She defensively explains:

> What do you do with a little one that has a problem like that . . . you just try to make him a complete person and that's very hard to do and of course in making him into a complete person you spend a lot of time with him and you can't let a baby stay in bed without talking to him and playing with him. He really had no activity outside . . . he wasn't like Teddy who I could get dressed and let him play out back in the sand box . . . so I would arrange these diversions . . . painting, drawing, and stories.

Characteristically, Mrs. Balasco links loss with unmet needs or dependency. Although she dominates this topic conversationally, Mr. Balasco, when asked how he felt, interjects:

> It was kind of tough. I used to come home from work at night and see him sitting there in his wheelchair.

Again, Mr. Balasco makes the familiar association between loss and helplessness or loss of power.

Thus, far, Davy seems to figure prominently in the Balascos' associations to loss and separation. On the eve of the last interview with the Balascos, Davy again became the focus of the discussion. On this occasion, Davy had been absent from home for two days without his parents' permission, and this unexpected separation, although emotionally trying for the Balascos, provided the investigator with an opportunity to observe their reactions to a current loss.

Tense and angry, Mr. Balasco forcefully dominates the discussion with remarks that primarily address his own shortcomings as a provider and a father. He states:

> And I thought that by me working there was enough money in and that I was doing my share and then we come into this and it gives you a long long look at what I have done wrong.

> The mistake lies with me . . . . I made it all along.

> The biggest mistake that I ever made especially with the two boys was not to clobber them until they couldn't walk.

As he experiences separation from his son, Mr. Balasco's thoughts and feelings seem to be colored with associations to personal and productive inadequacy as well as to powerlessness. As Mr. Balasco perseverates on the theme of inadequacy, Mrs. Balasco quietly ponders Davy's situation commenting:

> You know the thing that I'm afraid of with youngsters is that most of them carry no identification and you wonder . . . they could get into so much trouble, well not trouble, but an accident or something and you wouldn't know who they were that's what frightens me more than anything. Their father doesn't seem to worry about all of these things. I've been up since 12:45 this morning. I went to work at 6:00, but I kept getting sick to my stomach.

As Mrs. Balasco experiences separation from Davy, her thoughts turn to "an accident" and she seems in a way to be contemplating a permanent separation from Davy. Further along, she recalls actually responding to Davy's absence with physical illness. In this statement, Mrs. Balasco's illness is in her stomach, the body organ most frequently linked with loss and separation in her narrative. These associations are reminiscent of Mrs. Balasco's earlier recollection in which she connects the death of her brother, Alan, in a car accident with severe and enduring stomach problems. In the course of her remarks, Mrs. Balasco also contrasts her own involvement with her husband's seeming emotional isolation from the separation. Mr. Balasco underscores his wife's division of emotional labor when he asserts:

> My wife, she's the one. I know how my wife takes this. Ma really takes it hard, that's why a lot of times I don't even say nothing because if I should continue I'd drive her crazy. That's why I back off and keep quiet.

Here Mr. Balasco associatively reinforces the family myth that to speak of loss is to introduce an emotionally unmanageable topic. He restates the couple's emotionally isolative stance with regard to one another. He goes on to make a final association to the separation when he says:

> . . . not that I'm not mad, sure I'm mad but what am I to gain, a heart attack, and then what do I gain.

With this remark, Mr. Balasco connects powerlessness and a threat to his physical well-being with separation. Thus both parents seem to experience a separation from Davy as a severe threat to their well-being or survival.

In retrospect, the affective and cognitive associations to loss and separation which are foreground for the Balascos in their married and family life notably recapitulate salient associative themes from their respective families of origin. The narrative suggests that associative themes of dependency, helplessness, inadequacy, physical illness, emotional isolation, and threat to survival, contribute to the internal experience of loss and separation for Mr. and Mrs. Balasco, as well as dictating their respective behaviors and responses to these events. The data also illustrate the interactional potential of associative themes and suggest their importance in the determination of implicit and explicit relationships between and among family members.

As Davy's narrative is reviewed, a number of associative themes to loss and separation emerge, many of them bearing a strong resemblance to the motifs that play a prominent role in the association of his parents. In an early memory, Davy reconstructs the situation at home during a period when Mrs. Balasco was hospitalized for complications arising from her blood condition. He recalls:

> It was a huge house, it had 12 rooms and without my mother it looked like a shambles, the place went down the drain . . . because like my father came home from work and he didn't have time to clean and my sister was too little then, anyways she was going into the third or fourth grade you know, and I was stuck in a wheel chair and Teddy was just in the middle someplace and the house went.

Initially, Davy connects separation from his mother with a disruption and breakdown in the everyday working order of the house. His description of a deteriorating household in the absence of his mother resembles Mr. Balasco's reconstruction of the deteriorating farm in the absence of his siblings. A second dominant association is one of helplessness. Davy perceives himself as well as other family members as unable to bring order to the chaos caused by the loss. In particular, Davy connects his own helplessness with his physical disability, thus linking physical illness with separation. In general, Davy creates a picture of a family whose needs go unmet in the absence of the central female figure; like his mother, he associates loss and dependency. In overview, Davy conveys the feeling that although the loss is a temporary one, it presents a threat to the day-to-day existence of himself and the family.

Davy remembers that growing up he relied on his sister Christine a great deal and when she moved out of the house he notes:

> She left home and I didn't talk to a soul about my problems. After she left was a time when I started hibernating in my room, like I had no one to talk to.

Davy responds to the departure of his sister with emotional isolation. His association to "hibernating" suggests that he experiences the loss of his sister as a threat to his emotional survival. The associative link between separation and isolation appears again as Davy talks about his feelings regarding the family's recent move from one community to another. He resentfully states:

> I finally got to meeting friends down there and then I move here and I know no one and I got to stay here and there's nothing that I can do about it and what's the use.

In addition to isolation, Davy links helplessness to separation in this remark.

Davy asserts that the most painful loss that he has experienced is the death of his Aunt Lydia, approximately seven months prior to the inquiry. He explains:

> We were like this close . . . we'd always talk and she'd always take me out places and we'd always be doing stuff. I would have given up my life so she could have lived. I felt so rotten inside. My heart broke into a million pieces. I felt like dying and being buried next to her. I wanted to do something to bring her back.

The dominant association here seems to be the severe threat which the loss poses to Davy's emotional well-being. He implies that her loss was so emotionally overwhelming that he desired to die with her as he felt unable to tolerate the affect evoked by her absence. A second salient association is made between loss and helplessness.

In general, Davy seems to associate loss and separation with a threat to his emotional well-being or survival. This association is congruent with the underlying association to loss and separation made by both his parents. Furthermore, specific associations that are foreground for Davy, such as helplessness, dependency, isolation, disruption, and physical disability, recapitulate many of the associative themes which dominate the narratives of his parents as they speak about their families of origin, their marriage, and finally their family life. Davy's experiential rendering of loss and separation represents a blend of the affective and cognitive associations expressed by both Balascos, and illustrates the perpetuation of associative themes across generational boundaries. Most importantly, not only does this associative material signify a link with the emotional past but it represents a bond between and among family members within a particular sphere of family experience in the present.

Adolescent Findings

Although lacking the generational depth provided by the data from the Balasco family, the narratives of the adolescent participants are rich with cognitive and affective associations to loss and separation. As demonstrated with the Balascos, individuals may share basic meanings and affects about loss and separation, although the themes which unify these meanings and feelings may differ for each. The associative material gathered from the original six adolescent participants consisted of striking thematic contrasts; however, careful scrutiny of the material revealed that all six adolescents shared a basic experience with regard to loss and separation. The narrative material from the two adolescent participants included here is illustrative.

Nancy Franklin

Although Nancy recalls only one death in her extended family, her recollections of that loss are vivid. When she was 18, her paternal grandmother died. As she speaks of the loss, Nancy focuses mainly on the wake and the family's expectations that everyone attend. She adamantly states:

> I didn't want to go to the wake because I'm afraid of dead people. I mean you're looking at a dead person and I guess that it's the spirit or something, but it just feels like they're going to get up and start walking.

Here the primary association to loss and specifically death is fear. She implies that the dead are not really dead, or that loss is not final. Nancy admits that her fear of dead people was fostered in part by "my aunt, who used to tell me that when a person in the family dies, they're going to come after me." A dead relative, Nancy thus asserts, does not rest but instead poses a threat to her safety. Nancy angrily explains that her parents "forced" her to attend the wake. Before and after that event she had a dream in which her dead grandmother "used to come alive and come into my room and try to choke me." In the dream, Nancy links loss with violent physical injury. Once again, she does not feel safe in relation to loss. At the wake, Nancy recalls that her parents "dragged" her up to look at the body and she says, "I was scared and mad but I couldn't do anything about it." Along with anger and fear, Nancy connects loss with helplessness. Indeed, as she describes the wake, she paints a picture of victimization. She depicts herself at the mercy of her parents and her dead grandmother, as she is "forced," "dragged," and "choked," in this associative account of loss.

In early childhood, Nancy remembers an incident in which her pet gerbils were flushed down the toilet by her mother while Nancy was away at school. Angrily, Nancy recalls:

> It would be like if somebody picked me up and dumped me into a river . . . like if I was young and couldn't defend myself and I knew that somebody was going to hurt me.

Again Nancy links loss with feelings of helplessness and physical injury. Remembering her reaction when she returned home from school she says:

> I was mad and I went upstairs and started throwing things and I didn't talk to anybody for a month.

Here Nancy recalls explosive anger and muteness, implying that the affects which she experienced around loss were potent and unspeakable, and emotionally isolating.

At age 16, Nancy was separated from her family when she entered a hospital for an operation on her arm. She relates her most vivid memory of the experience:

> They strapped me down to the table and they took a white sheet and put it over my head, like this person is dead, they've got to put a sheet over her head.

The dominant association in this memory of her separation from her family seems to be one to death itself. Concurrently, Nancy experiences feelings of helplessness ("they strapped me down").

As Nancy talks about her two successive abortions, which occurred approximately a year prior to the inquiry, she remembers feeling "quite depressed" and admits, "I feel that someday, something is going to happen to me for doing it." In addition to the association of depression, Nancy links retribution with loss.

In summary, several associative themes are dramatically represented in Nancy's narrative. She repeatedly associates loss with a threat to her safety asserting a concrete belief in the return of the dead and implying on a more abstract level that loss is not final and that the living are helpless when confronted with the affects and cognitions associated with loss. Nancy's associations of fear, violence, and physical injury are subsumed under a second major associative theme, that of retribution. Both her fear for her safety and her fear of retribution suggest that Nancy associates loss with a threat to her very survival.

Linda Petite

Linda Petite articulates a narrative rich in references to loss and separation. The associations in the sequential excerpts from the following dialogue are representative of some of the themes which dominate her cognitive and affective experience of loss and separation. The dialogue begins as Linda tearfully reflects on feelings of loneliness:

Linda: I don't like to feel lonely. Sometimes I think that is why I can't cry at wakes or funerals because of the loneliness of the person who's dead. I just think that to feel sorry for someone who's dead is like saying it's ok to feel loneliness.

Interviewer: Do you sometimes feel that you are as lonely as someone who's dead?

Linda: Um hum. Sometimes I just feel like I'm the only person in the world and that these are people that I've created in my mind . . . that I'm not really living, it's only a dream and that I wish I would wake up from my dream.

In the initial part of this interchange, Linda associates death and loneliness. She explains that to allow herself to experience the affect associated with loss, is to feel the loneliness which she links with death. Thus, there is an implication that she connects loss with emotional isolation and that the affects linked with loss and separation pose a considerable threat to her emotional survival. Linda goes on to make further associations to loss:

Linda: Death doesn't scare me, it's the way I'll go that scares me.

Interviewer: What is it about the way that you'll go that scares you?

Linda   Pain, I don't like pain.

Interviewer: You mentioned earlier that there's a history of cancer in your family.

Linda: That scares me.

Interviewer: Are you afraid that it will happen to you?

Linda: Yes.

Interviewer: Are other members of your family afraid of that happening to them?

Linda: No . . . well my Aunt Brigitte was just cured of leukemia but she had cancer and my Aunt Madilyn had cancer but it was taken out and my mother doesn't have it but sometimes I worry she will . . . it scares me, cancer scares me. It's not the disease that scares me, it's the pain.

Here Linda confesses fear about the pain which she connects with separating from others (i.e., "the way I'll go"). As she recounts a partial history of the occurrence of cancer in her extended family, associative links appear between cancer and women, specifically her mother and her maternal aunts as well as herself. Finally, coming a full associative circle, Linda links cancer with fear and again fear with pain. Thus, Linda seems to make a cognitive link between being a female in her family, contracting cancer, and the threat of painful separation. The specific association of Mrs. Petite, cancer, and the threat of loss appears again in the concluding portion of the discussion as Linda explains her reaction to occasional illnesses suffered by her mother:

Linda: Every so often she'll get really sick like with the flu and then she'll be ok and other than that my mother hasn't been sick.

Interviewer: Do you get frightened when she's sick?

Linda: Yeah.

Interviewer: What are you frightened of?

Linda: Well not cancer . . . that she has cancer, but that she's just lying around. Sometimes I even visualize her being dead.

Interviewer: What's that like?

Linda: I feel that if she dies I'll have a lot of responsibility and I won't be able to do things because I'd have to be like a mother to my sister and my brother and my father and sometimes I get angry when she's sick and sometimes I like the feeling of having the responsibility.

With these comments, Linda makes a direct association between loss and her mother. The associative consequences of such a loss are increased responsibility for Linda within the family context and concurrent restraints on her personal freedom. Finally, she associates feelings of ambivalence to loss, describing an alternating experience of anger and gratification. Linda's crying and labored speech throughout the interchange further suggest the emotional strain which she connects with loss.

A broad review of the material in these three excerpts illuminates Linda's tendency to equate fear of loss with death itself. She admits to occasionally thinking of her mother as dead. Moreover, she reflects upon her own vitality in uncertain terms ("Sometimes I just feel like I'm the only person in the world . . . that I'm not really living, it's only a dream"). As Linda feels loneliness or separateness from others, she experiences herself as dead. These sentiments are succinctly stated by Linda in a remark about a close friend who recently left for the West Coast:

> Then there's this friend of mine. I know she's still living, but to me she's dead.

Although angry at her friend before her departure, Linda admits that :

> The straw that broke the camel's back was that she left without even saying good-bye . . . she didn't even call to say good-bye.

In these remarks about her friend, Linda first equates separation with death and secondly connects loss with not having the opportunity to say good-bye, thus implying that she feels affectively cheated. This latter associative theme occurs repeatedly throughout Linda's narrative.

In summary, the associative link between pain and loss and separation seems to play a dominant role in Linda's narrative. Within the cognitive realm, she associates pain to cancer and cancer to the threat of loss of the female members in her family. Linda's affective presentation of this material suggests that she experiences loss and separation as painfully overwhelming events that evoke feelings of extreme isolation, fear, anger, and ambiivalence. Her equation of loss and separation with death further underscores the associative link between loss and isolation. In short, the associative material implies that Linda experiences loss and separation as a serious threat to her emotional well-being.

Summary of Family and Adolescent Findings

A retrospective glance at the associative data recorded in this chapter brings to mind the wide range of affective and cognitive themes which are foreground for the Balasco family and the adolescent participants in their recollections of loss and separation. However, while the themes which bind the associations are diverse, the associations themselves are held together by a common meaning. All the participants in the inquiry cognitively and affectively experience loss and separation as a serious threat. More specifically, each participant, in his or her own way, attributes potent, enduring, and unmanageable qualities to these events and acknowledges the potentially disruptive and overwhelming effect that loss and separation can have on their day-to-day existence. Furthermore, an overview of the findings also suggests that the participants often equate the experience of separation with loss itself. In short, separation as well as loss are experienced on the most basic level as a threat to survival.

5

Identifying Relationship Patterns

This chapter will examine the way in which the special meanings that the participants attribute to loss and separation influence relationships in their day-to-day
lives. The focus here will be on the identification of relationship patterns in the
families of the participants. An analysis of the purpose and meaning of these
relationship patterns will be undertaken in the following chapter.

In its attempt to identify the qualitative and structural dimensions which
characterize the relationships of the participants, the discussion will consider the
interview material from three perspectives. Each of these perspectives reflects a
different degree of abstraction in the relating process. The first and most highly
abstract perspective is a dialectical one which recognizes the complementary roles
played by separation and closeness in the process of relation. The second viewpoint is one which addresses how separation and closeness are represented
thematically within the context of relationships. Finally, the third and most
concrete perspective is one which traces these themes to their manifestations in
behavior and interaction.

From the Hegelian point of view, a dialectic refers to a process of change in
which "an entity passes over and is preserved and fulfilled by its opposite"
(Webster, 1970). It is a process which involves the development of phenomena
through the stages of thesis, antithesis, and synthesis. Thus, within a dialectical
framework, a phenomenon cannot be viewed or understood without consideration
of its opposite or counterpart. Viewed dialectically, relationships may be seen as
the resolution or synthesis of the antithetical forces of separation and closeness.
Nagy (1973) stresses the interplay between these forces in relationships when he
states:

> . . . separation, separateness, otherness, or difference recognized in their antithetical dynamic
> balance with closeness . . . constitute a vital force. On the other hand, taken in an absolute sense,
> they resemble the peaceful quiet ultimately offered by the cemetery.(p. 22)

From a dialectical perspective, interpersonal distance, or relationship, can be
considered simultaneously in terms of distance or separateness, and in terms of

proximity or closeness. The dynamic balance of a relationship system may be envisioned as the extent to and manner in which relating individuals move towards or away from one another. The structural and qualitative dimensions of a relationship system, provide important information about the system's dynamic balance. For example, within a family relationship system, the over-involvement of the parents with one of many children will represent a different dynamic balance within the system than the parents' more diffuse involvement with all of the children. In short, because it provides a model which stresses the role of separation in the relating process, the dialectical approach proves useful in the consideration of data involving the effect of separation and loss on relationship formation and direction.

Some of the phenomenological constructs of Kantor's (1975) theory have proven useful in bridging the gap from the abstract dialectial forces to their manifestations in thematic material and, finally, in interaction. Generally, Kantor's theory systematically aims at studying interaction within the family system. A cornerstone of his theory is the concept of distance regulation or how family members deal with interpersonal distance. Although his theory does not address the dialectical nature of relationships, Kantor does provide constructs which delineate the thematic fields in which relationships take place and the manner in which these themes can be traced to interaction. The thematic fields or experiential dimensions in which Kantor grounds relational activity are those of "Meaning," "Affect," and "Power." Kantor's contructs point out that distance can not only be conceptualized in quantitative terms such as space and time, but can also be thought of as the way individuals move towards or away from one another in conceptual, emotional, and volitional fields. Distance within these latter dimensions can be conceptualized cumulatively as "relational" rather than "physical" distance.

The field of "Meaning" encompasses the conceptual experience of family members, or the way in which they regulate interpersonal distance using ideologies, values, and beliefs. For example, family members may rely on shared beliefs in order to build group unity and cohesiveness, or at other times may rely on differing beliefs to attain and experience separateness from the family group. The field of "Affect" embodies the emotional experience of family members. In this dimension, family members use feelings as a way to move towards or away from one another. For example, family members may express and share particular sentiments in an attempt to achieve group closeness, or may experience and articulate diverse feelings in an attempt to seek individuality and separateness. The dimension of "Power" encompasses the volitional experience of a family system. Volition within a system involves the allocation of leadership and decision-making in the service of system goal attainment. A family system may seek to attain its goals by allocating power or leadership to one family member or by allocating power to numerous family members who then have the option of choosing to make decisions for the system as a whole or for themselves as individual family members. Kantor stresses that the thematic fields of "Meaning," "Affect," and "Power" are not mutually exclusive and that family members may choose to move towards or away from one another within one, two, or all three fields simultaneously. Kantor goes on to point out that it is from these fields that the rules or expectations regarding behavior and interaction within the family system stem. For example, a family in which a primary goal is group intimacy may create a family rule which states that the affect-laden experiences of all family members must be shared each evening at the dinner table.

The present discussion strives to unify its dialectical, thematic, and interactional approaches to the data through the notion of the dialogue. The dialogue is a concept which Nagy borrows from Buber. It refers, on the dyadic level, to the dynamic exchange between an individual and his or her relational counterpart and, on the systemic level, to the on-going process of change and redefinition that occurs as the system and its members interact. In short, the dialogue represents the continuous process of individual and systemic definition which is based in the subjective experience of those involved in interaction. The dynamic balance of a relationship system is perpetually in a state of flux. This state of flux is reflected in qualitative and structural shifts in the system. The notion of the dialogue as it will be used in this discussion requires further elaboration of Nagy's concept. Here, the dialogue between an individual and his or her family system will refer to the manifestation in interaction of the themes associated with the dialectical forces involved in the relating process. Specifically, interactional and behavioral rules may be conceptualized as stemming from the salient themes which the participants and their families link with the antithetical forces of separation or loss and closeness.

The interview material in chapter 4 reveals that the participants hold a shared meaning with regard to events of loss and separation; they view the possibility of these events as threatening to their day-to-day existence. In retrospect, this shared meaning was derived from specific sets of conceptual, affective, and volitional themes which the participants associated with loss and separation in their narratives. Speculatively, in light of these findings, these individuals might be expected to maximize closeness or proximity, or minimize relational as well as physical distance. This "distance minimization" hypothesis can be examined by delineating the salient relational patterns of the participants and their families through the identification of systemic dialogues.

The discussion will begin by examining the familial relationships of the participants for themes associated with closeness and viewing them in their relationship to themes associated with separation and loss. An examination of these themes will lead to a delineation of the interactional rules which organize and determine family behavior. With the identification of these family dialogues, the discussion will further examine systemic relationships, focusing more specifically on their qualitative and structural characteristics with the hope of addressing the manner in which shared meanings associated with separation and closeness, respectively, shape the relating process. Special attention will be given to the family's dialogue during the period of adolescence as it is during this time that shifts in systemic relationships are most likely to manifest themselves. In chapter 4, it was noted that the participants seem to equate the experience of separation with the experience of loss. Thus, the text to follow will use the term "separation" to refer to both experiences.

The discussion will begin by examining the narratives of the Balascos and their descriptions of familial relationships that span three generations. As these relationships are explored, both the long-term systemic goal of minimization of familial distance and the role which the family's dialogue plays in the attainment of this goal will become apparent.

Family Findings

The Balascos: Families of Origin

Mrs. Balasco describes her family of origin in a manner which suggests that relational distance was kept at a minimum. She recalls that "my mother and father really kind of lived for each other . . . they were both home people," and stresses that the number of physically disabled children in the family contributed to closeness. The following interview segment with Mrs. Balasco is illustrative:

Interviewer: There were a lot of children to take care of in the family.

Mrs. Balasco: Yes, that's why I think that we were such a close family. You know you don't think about these things until you sit down talking like this about it . . . I guess it really kept us very close . . . like even our mother never really let us go out a lot on our own.

Interviewer: Do you think that that had anything to do with Alan?

Mrs. Balasco: Yes . . . I never really thought about it growing up, but I'm sure this is why my mother kept us kind of close. I'm sure that my kids don't realize the kind of things you are trying to teach them growing up until they're older. My mother probably had some type of fear that something would happen to us.

Interviewer: What types of things wouldn't she let you do?

Mrs. Balasco: Well, I don't remember that she wouldn't let us do any particular thing. Of course we were all very contented at home . . . we all got along good—played a lot of games. My mother was a very interesting person. She was very good with her hands—good at sewing, knitting—she really kept us interested in a lot of different things. But now that I'm older, and I think about it, maybe some of the things that she did was to keep us at home. Like when we went out, we stayed in the yard . . . we weren't allowed to play in the street. Unconsciously, I never thought about it until now but I never let my kids play in the street either.

Here, Mrs. Balasco implies that relational and physical distance among family members, particularly her mother and the children, was not tolerated well. The children were kept "kind of close" and both directly and indirectly discouraged from going out on their own. A second recollection accentuates the difficulty which Mrs. Balasco's mother had tolerating distance between herself and her children. Mrs. Balasco recalls:

> My mother never went out without taking two or three of us. We didn't have a car so we would walk, and she would take my brother and I or my sister or usually all three of us.

This memory further substantiates the minimization of distance between Mrs. Balasco's mother and her children. In these sequential recollections, she is remembered as being with them both inside and outside of the home. Mrs. Balasco's account of her mother's response to the permanent institutionalization of her daughter, Evelyn, at age 13, is noteworthy as it makes an even more encompassing implication about relationship patterns in her family of origin. Mrs. Balasco explains:

> My mother never went to visit her because she said she couldn't; if she ever went to visit her she knew she would bring her home.

Illustrated here are two extremes of relational distance. Mrs. Balasco implies that her mother's relationship with Evelyn can only be managed on an all or none basis. Either her mother maintains a very close relationship with Evelyn in the home, or she never sees her, opting for extreme distance. A "visit" or a compromise distance cannot be tolerated. In this instance, the alternatives for relational distance between Mrs. Balasco's mother and Evelyn are severely limited and are bipolar in nature.

Mr. Balasco's recollections of his family of origin also point out the consistent minimization of distance as he depicts family members staying close to home. These memories are illustrative:

> Of course my mother didn't go to the hospital to have babies, she had them all at home.

> We were never allowed to go and visit too many people, we never really left the farm.

> You didn't go too far, you made your friends close by so you could be home.

Mr. Balasco's vivid memory of his unfulfilled desire to spend the summer in Puerto Rico playing baseball underscores the family's intolerance of both physical and relational distance and, specifically, highlights the tenacious hold which Mr. Balasco's father had on him.

Mr. Balasco: I wanted to play baseball in the worst way . . . I had an arm on me, I could pitch forever, but I was a farm boy and that was all I knew, work.

Interviewer: So there were a lot of things that you were never able to do?

Mr. Balasco: Yeah . . . I played a bit of local ball and the coach said I was so good that he wanted to send me to Puerto Rico for the summer to play. Jesus, can you imagine me going back and telling my father. If I said to my father that I wanted to play ball, he would say "play ball, see those weeds over there."

Interviewer: So there were some things that you weren't allowed to do?

Mr. Balasco: Right . . . I just kept farming, farming . . . it didn't phase me, it couldn't.

Interviewer: So you're saying that you never had time to get upset because you were so busy working?

Mr. Balasco: That's right. But you know inside of me I always wanted to go.

Interviewer: How did you deal with those feelings?

Mr. Balasco: I took the negative side . . . I probably wouldn't make it . . . then another thing that did bother me was that I would have to leave my mother and she just got so upset when my brother had gone away and being close to the family I didn't want to break a tie. But I could throw a ball . . . but you know I never forgot this. It was one of the big highlights of my life . . . once I asked my father to watch me play ball . . . boy, what a goddamn beating I got that night.

Mr. Balasco's feelings that a temporary separation for the summer would constitute "breaking a tie," and his reluctance to do this suggests his adherence to the family pattern of distance minimization. Other remarks in his narrative, such as "I'm not partial to busting things up," further illustrate this tendency. After recounting the beating that he received for even playing ball locally, Mr. Balasco goes on to reflect:

> You know, it's amazing to me that the way that we were brought up we didn't become Jesse James . . . you know if he was around when we were growing up we would have joined him. What more did we have but the farm.

As he remembers the inflexibility of his family in permitting either physical or relational distance, Mr. Balasco fantasizes about running away with an outlaw. Here, two extreme patterns of distance are conceptually juxtaposed. Either Mr. Balasco remains spatially, volitionally, and conceptually "tied" to the farm and continues to work, or he rebels and joins up with an outlaw who notably steals rather than works for a living. The alternatives for establishing distance presented here are limited and have a bipolar quality. As suggested earlier, a compromise distance represented as playing baseball in Puerto Rico for one summer is not negotiable.

Thus far, the data highlights a pattern which minimizes distance among family members in the families of both Mr. and Mrs. Balasco. The families' seemingly rigid adherence to this pattern often precludes the attainment of compromise distances; the families' repertoire of physical and relational distance patterns is frequently limited to bipolar choices.

The major patterns of relational distance delineated for the Balascos' respective families of origin are illustrated further and, in addition, more specific relational patterns are identified as Mr. and Mrs. Balasco describe relationships that transpire as their siblings encounter adolescence. Adolescence is a period of growth during which children are presented with both societal and familial expectations that they assume increasing responsibility for themselves and, in so doing, initiate a more autonomous relationship with their families, and in particular their parents. This movement away from the family, which is acknowledged as the developmental task of adolescence in many theories (A. Freud, 1946; Erickson, 1950; and Blos, 1962) can be viewed as a "transactional process" that involves both parents and children (Stierlin, 1974). This process tests the mutual abilities of the parents and the adolescents to initiate, tolerate, and accept conceptual, emotional, and volitional differences, or an increase in relational distance. Ideally, this developmental task is accomplished when the adolescent and his or her parents negotiate a relational distance which signifies an experience of acceptable separateness for both or, as Stierlin states, which "leads to relative independence for both parties, yet is an independence based upon mature interdependence." Presumably, families that stress minimal relational distance will experience difficulty as the children reach adolescence; the negotiation of distance will prove problematic for both parents and the adolescent children. Relevant examples from the narratives of Mr. and Mrs. Balasco substantiate this assumption.

Mr. Balasco's description of the manner in which his oldest sibling, Robert, departs from the family is illustrative:

Mr. Balasco: The first one to leave was Bobby, the oldest. He went away to school. He was a linguist. My father eked out a living on this farm, a mere existence, and put this boy through Cornell and about four more colleges and he became a linguist.

Interviewer: How did the family feel about that?

Mr. Balasco: Oh, my father and mother were upset because in a Portuguese family, the oldest boy is either supposed to be a god . . . some sort of god . . . either a priest, a lawyer, or a judge, they want him in that category. They hoped at least that he would come home and with all his education take over the farm and take care of us. But he never did. He was down there (i.e., South America) for 30 years . . . and when he came back he was an alcoholic and he didn't care about the farm.

Initially, Robert adheres to his family's pattern of distance minimization by attending college and thereby meeting the ethnic expectation that the oldest boy receive an education. However, his ultimate career choice represents a deviation from the rigid professional expectations that characterize the family's ethnic background. Thus, Robert attains increased conceptual distance from his family by countering predominant ethnic values. His choice to live at an extreme distance constitutes another challenge to the family's belief system which holds that the children are supposed to remain close to home. Finally, Robert's refusal to assume responsibility for the farm upon his return signifies a continued defiance of the ethnic expectations which help bind relational distance in the family. Robert's actions also suggest that he attains increased volitional distance from his family. He is able to mobilize enough individual power to make decisions apart from the wishes of his parents. However, Robert's dependence on alcohol suggests that he is less successful in the attainment of emotional distance. As viewed within the context of the rigid values and authoritarian parental stance which contribute to the process of distance minimization in his family, Robert's attempts to gain increased relational distance seem extreme, but necessary, given the family's previously illustrated intolerance of relative increases in distance. As Robert encounters and passes through adolescence, neither he nor members of his family are able to negotiate a compromise distance at which mutual and acceptable difference is experienced. Thus, the options for attaining relational distance are limited and again take on a bipolar quality. In short, the only way for Robert to experience himself as different is to attempt to become extremely different. Notably as he moves to an extreme relational distance, he is no longer accepted by his family as the following remarks made by Mr. Balasco suggest:

> Nobody knew him anyway . . . he was an odd duck . . . he never did get along with any of us when he came back.

Mr. Balasco's recollection of his sister Carol's departure from the farm to "marry an Irishman, an act that was almost against the Portuguese dynasty," again illustrates an attempt by an adolescent family member to achieve increased relational distance in the conceptual and volitional realms through defiance of rigid ethnic and parental expectations. As he describes his sister's choice, its extreme aspects are notable and reminiscent once more of the limited options available for attaining distance in Mr. Balasco's family of origin.

Mr. Balasco's account of his older brother John's leavetaking particularly highlights the family's inability to *negotiate* relational distance. Mr. Balasco recalls:

> John had a fight with my father . . . he had just turned 18 or 20 and he wanted to go play ball in the afternoon with the fellows. And my father said, "You milk the cows." And he says, "Well you're not telling me" and my father says, "Well, there's the door."

Here, both father and son are involved in a scenario which accentuates the limited distance options available to family members, and exemplifies again their difficulty in negotiating the developmental task of adolescence.

In summary, Mr. Balasco's account suggests that the negotiation of mutually "acceptable separateness" between parents and adolescent children was extremely problematic in his family of origin. The examples recorded here highlight the limited distance choices available to the family and its adolescent children as they attempt to orchestrate the separation process.

As Mrs. Balasco speaks about her family and describes the growth of her siblings, references to strivings for increased relational distance are notably absent. A majority of her siblings were physically disabled. Doubtless, this fact made the attainment of autonomy more difficult and, on some occasions, impossible, as exemplified by Mrs. Balasco's sister Evelyn, and later, her sister Gail, both of whom were permanently institutionalized. However, her description of the manner in which George, one of the few "healthy" children left home, is reminiscent of the salient distancing processes utilized by the adolescent members of Mr. Balasco's family. Mrs. Balasco recalls that for approximately one and a half years after the death of her mother, she bore a significant portion of the responsibility for the family with her brother George. She remembers how they both shared chores, such as washing clothes, and how they both held part-time jobs after school to contribute to the family income. Mrs. Balasco admits, "We had quite a responsibility as far as the kids go." Abruptly, at age 16, George dropped out of high school and enlisted in the Army to be stationed in Japan and Germany for several years. Mrs. Balasco speculates, "I guess he felt that he had to get away." Looking back, George initially participates in the family task of minimizing distance by meeting parental expectations; he remains at home and allows other members of the family to depend on him. Along with Mrs. Balasco, he occupies the role of primary caretaker in the family. However, his abrupt rejection of these responsibilities challenges the family's conceptual and volitional expectations. Both his sudden leavetaking and the physical distance to which he travels preclude any possibility of his continued participation in the family's interaction. George's actions are sudden and extreme in nature and suggest that negotiation of a compromise distance is not possible in his family.

In retrospect, the siblings referred to in the Balascos' respective families approach the developmental work of adolescence by refusing to participate in the mutually acknowledged family task of distance minimization. Specifically, each achieves increased relational distance by declining to take part in the family interaction associated with this task. Thus, as these adolescents move away from their families they are decreasing the intensity with which they are involved in the "dialogues" of their respective family systems. In order to provide a more specific context within which the separation of these adolescents, as well as the separation of other members of the Balascos' respective families, can be understood, it is necessary to define more clearly the dialogues particular to each family. To review briefly, a family's dialogue is the manifestation in interaction of the dialectical elements—separateness and closeness—involved in relationship formation and change. The interactional rules or expectations which contribute to the dialogue are based on the salient conceptual, emotional, and volitional themes which a family attaches to closeness and separation. Identifying the dialogues for the Balascos' families of origin involves delineating these themes and tracing their contribution to family interaction. Examples from the narratives of the Balascos in this and the previous chapter are helpful in illuminating the dialogues in which members of their respective families engage.

In the preceding chapter, specific associative themes are foreground for the Balascos as they speak about loss and separation. For Mr. Balasco these associative themes include powerlessness, emotional and physical vulnerability, deterioration, and productivity in both its barren and fertile phases. For Mrs. Balasco these themes include physical disability, emotional and cognitive inadequacy, and dependency. Embedded in the Balascos' descriptive examples recorded thus far in this chapter are themes or motifs associated with closeness in their respective families. In Mr. Balasco's family these motifs include authority or power, possession of physical and emotional stamina, and perpetuation of the family's ethnic and occupational (i.e., as farmers) identities. In Mrs. Balasco's family these themes include physical health, emotional and cognitive adequacy, assuming responsibility, and caretaking. A joint consideration within each family of the themes associated with separation and those associated with closeness reveals the complementarity of the motifs. As family members relate to one another, they do so using rules, meeting behavioral expectations, and assuming behavioral postures derived from these themes. These complementary behavioral postures constitute the family dialogue. If, indeed, the families of the participants strive to minimize intrafamilial distance, the family dialogue would serve in the accomplishment of this goal. That is, family interaction is directed at perpetuating closeness or behavioral complementarity and minimizing separateness (i.e., separation) or conflict. Crisis within the relationship system occurs when a behavioral posture or a set of behavioral expectations is amplified or intensified to a point at which the potential for complementarity with another posture or set of expectations decreases or is precluded. Thus, the dynamic balance of a family relationship system is determined by the extent to and manner in which family members adhere to interactional rules, fulfill behavioral expectations, and assume behavioral postures. Substantial conflict has the potential to alter the balance of interactional forces, disrupt the family dialogue, and, ultimately, threaten the survival of the system (i.e., fragment or terminate systemic relationships, thereby threatening the efficacy of family functioning).

Speculatively, family members are involved in the family dialogue in varying degrees. For example, a parent might be solely responsible for a type of behavior or behavioral stance (e.g., decision-making), while many family members might share in the generation of a complementary behavioral posture (e.g., accepting the decision). Thus, the actual loss of a family member could constitute a significant disruption to the system depending on the importance of that family member's contribution to the family dialogue. The vacating of an important role in the dialogue by one family member would necessitate the substitution of another family member(s) in that position. Thus, a serious disruption in a family's dialogue would require a rebalancing of the family's relationship system. The success of a rebalancing effort depends on the family's ability to compensate for the disruption, or to eliminate crisis by adequately restoring behavioral complementarity.

It is against this backdrop that the drama of adolescent separation takes place. The adolescent siblings referred to thus far in the Balascos' narratives establish relational distance from their respective families by decreasing their involvement in the family dialogue. The individual choices of Robert, Carol, and John contradict the rules of family interaction. These adolescents refuse to meet the interactional expectations associated with closeness (i.e., carrying on the family's ethnic and occupational identities) and those associated with separation (i.e., powerlessness). Similarly, George's departure from home represents his decreased involvement in his family's dialogue as he opposes interactional expectations by refusing to be a caretaker and by refusing to be a sick, inadequate family member. Although these adolescents achieve increased relational distance from their families, the sensitivity of their respective family systems to the disruptive threat posed by loss makes the task of separation difficult to negotiate and necessitates the choice of relatively extreme distancing mechanisms. However, the mutual ability of the adolescents and their families to allow and, to some degree, to tolerate the separation suggests that the roles played by these adolescents in the maintenance of the family dialogue was initially less important than the roles played by other family members. Undoubtedly, the separation of these adolescents results in a need to rebalance or adjust systemic relationships; however, it does not seem to substantially interfere with the family task of distance minimization and, consequently, does not pose a serious threat to the survival of the system.

In contrast to these adolescents are the siblings in the Balascos' respective families of origin who play important roles in the family dialogue. In this category are the extremely sick or physically vulnerable children. Examples in Mrs. Balasco's family of origin include Jimmy, Evelyn, and Gail, all of whom comply with interactional rules associated with an important aspect of the family dialogue. As sick and excessively needy children, they fulfill expectations that complement the caretaking role of other family members. Mrs. Balasco noted earlier in her narrative that it was caring for the sick children that kept the family "close." Notably the family is forced to confront separation from both Evelyn and Gail as these two children reach a point at which they comply with a set of behavioral expectations so rigidly that the potential for complementary interaction from other family members is eliminated. That is, Evelyn and Gail become too sick and too needy and other family members can no longer care for them—the dialogue between these children and the family is terminated and their impact disrupts the system. Evelyn's separation from the family at age 13 particularly illustrates this point and proves most disruptive for Mrs. Balasco's mother. Because she can no longer care for Evelyn in an all-consuming manner, Mrs. Balasco's mother never goes to see Evelyn once she has been institutionalized. Here, interaction between mother and daughter comes to an abrupt halt.

An example of a physically vulnerable child in Mr. Balasco's family of origin is his brother Peter. Crippled at an early age by polio, Peter lacks the physical stamina and productive capacity that characterizes other family members. Peter's inadequacies complement the characteristics of other family members who are physically strong productive farm workers. As Mr. Balasco implies earlier in his narrative, it is farming and its implicit meaning—helping things grow—that keeps his family close. The deaths of Michael and Paul, the two infants who preceded Mr. Balasco in the birth order, constitute a disruptive loss to the family system. As growing children, they meet certain behavioral expectations (i.e., they are family members who Mr. Balasco's parents can help grow) which contribute to the complementarity of the family dialogue. Their deteriorating health and ultimate deaths signal an amplification of a behavioral posture which, in turn, eliminates the possibility for complementarity within the realm of family interaction.

Notably, each of the Balascos' families of origin needs family members who will meet interactional expectations associated with separation in order to maintain the complementarity upon which the family bases its dialogue. However, amplification of these interactions gives way to fixed or static positions that no longer complement the behavioral positions of other family members, thus disrupting the family dialogue and threatening the survival of the relationship system.

Thus far, the separations between children and parents which occur in the Balascos' respective families of origin seem to fall at opposite ends of a continuum. At one end is the willful separation which transpires as a result of the child's developmentally appropriate oppostion to parental expectations. As they separate from the family, children in this category decrease the extent to which family interactional rules dictate their behaviors. At the other end of the continuum is the unwillful separation which takes place when a child inadvertantly amplifies parental behavioral expectations associated with separation. Children in this group eliminate the potential for complementary behavior from other family members, thereby disrupting the family dialogue and terminating their role in it. In short, at one end of the continuum is the child who through separation seeks an identity that differs from his or her parents. At the opposite end is the child who through separation negates an identity apart from his or her parents entirely. All of these children assume some role in the family dialogue and in the accomplishment of the family's distance minimization goal. A review of the data to this point suggests that the children who separate unwillfully cause a greater disruption to the system and thus appear to have made a more significant contribution to the family dialogue.

An examination of the Balascos' relationships before, during, and after adolescence illuminates their contribution to their respective family dialogues and, in addition, provides more specific information about the contributions of other family members. Of note, as the Balascos recount their childhood and adolescence, there is a marked absence of either the volitional and conceptual opposition to behavioral expectations that facilitated the separation process for some of their siblings or the amplification of behavioral expectations that resulted in the unwillful separation of others. The Balascos and their respective parents neither initiate the process of separation nor passively submit to it.

Mr. Balasco: Family of Origin

At age 17, Mr. Balasco leaves the farm to join the "good old Navy." Mr. Balasco's leavetaking does not challenge familial expectations, but rather complies with them. For Mr. Balasco, the Navy denotes a home away from home. It embodies the values of strength, endurance, and hard work which were primary expectations within his family. In addition, the Navy's emphasis on regimentation and its general discouragement of individual differences recapitulates the minimization of relational distance stressed in Mr. Balasco's family. The following comments extracted from various portions of Mr. Balasco's narrative underscore the similarities between his family and the Navy:

> Life on the farm was like we were institutionalized or in the Service military-wise . . . everybody worked . . . it was regimented.

> I recall the day that I was going into the Service. My father said, "They're going to make a man out of you" and I said, "Pa, you have already done that in spades."

> All the time that I was in the Service, I was happy 'cause I had already had a background of being a Service man with what I had at home.

> When I was in the Service, I was so goddamn regimented that I was better than the other guys.

By joining the Navy, Mr. Balasco perpetuates values and beliefs that are salient for his family. As Mr. Balasco decides to leave and join the Service, there is a marked lack of opposition from his parents—there is no disagreement, no fighting, no conflict, and no tears. Parents and son are in mutual agreement. Mr. Balasco's choice to leave and join the Navy thus does not seem to challenge the conceptual, emotional, or volitional expectations or rules which constitute the family dialogue. Although physical space separates Mr. Balasco from his parents, he maintains proximity in relational space. That is, by continuing to comply with parental expectations, Mr. Balasco minimizes relational distance between himself and his parents.

After a number of years in the Navy, Mr. Balasco decided to return home. He recalls:

> . . . in the Service I came up through the ranks . . . I got to know the Lieutenant Commander on my ship who said to me, "Why you going home? You're first class now. I'll help promote you." I said, "Na, I want to go home and see my father and do a little farming."

Mr. Balasco's decision to return home in the face of a promotion underscores his commitment to remain involved in the family dialogue at the expense of pursuing his own identity separate from the family. His return to what he had described earlier as a "deteriorated farm" to "do a little farming" implies a strong investment in the perpetuation of the family's occupational identity. However, as Mr. Balasco works on the farm during this period of time, he recalls trying to support a wife and child on practically no income:

> I was working on the farm and I was paying nine dollars a week for rent and I couldn't even afford that. I was on on-the-job training from the government and they were paying me 90 bucks a month and my father figured that that was all I should get paid but he was supposed to match what Uncle Sam gave me but he couldn't quite . . . and I stuck this out for three years.

Mr. Balasco's choice to work on the farm in spite of the fact that his father does not pay him represents his compliance with the family's conceptual and volitional rules. Mr. Balasco's earlier references to his childhood years in which he alluded to himself and his siblings as "work horses" and as "a working machine" suggest that within his family being a child meant providing free labor. He notes:

> The reason for all of us leaving was to make something better for ourselves. Even if it was farming we were going to get paid . . . My father always had a great saying: "I'm doing this all for you." He didn't realize that if he added the whole thing up that we bought the goddamn place. But this is the ethnic group, they're all this way, not just my father, all of them. They brought you into this world and they figured from then on you must carry. Of course, I was always the type of fellow that I liked farming so much that I could care less . . . the money didn't bother me.

Here, Mr. Balasco finally admits that although his siblings left the family to "get paid," he alone was willing to remain on the farm and work. Mr. Balasco's enthusiasm for farming and his willingness to work for free illustrates his commitment to maintaining the complementarity of the family dialogue. As an unpaid "workhorse," Mr. Balasco recapitulates a childhood position which provides an interactional complement to the authoritarian, overseer stance of his father. This and other examples from the narrative suggest that Mr. Balasco's contribution to the family dialogue differs notably from that of his siblings, both in terms of quality and duration. Mr. Balasco's reluctance to oppose parental expectations interferes with the achievement of the parent-child separation associated with adolescence. At the same time, Mr. Balasco's ability to avoid amplifying the behavioral posture which his family links to separation helps to protect him from a permanent and unconditional separation from his parents. Thus, Mr. Balasco continues to be an important participant in family interaction. Speculatively, it is both his ability to meet behavioral expectations connected to closeness (e.g., perpetuating the family identity as farmers) and his ability and willingness to at times follow behavioral rules associated with separation (e.g., allowing himself to assume a powerless position on the farm) which makes his contribution to family interaction both an important and much needed one. Mr. Balasco's adeptness at shifting his behavioral posture within the family system allows him and his parents to achieve the interactional complementarity necessary for the perpetuation of the family dialogue. Thus, Mr. Balasco's significant role in minimizing distance in the family appears to have a detrimental effect on his capacity to establish relational distance between himself and his parents.

As long as he remains on the farm, Mr. Balasco strives with his parents to sustain behavior complementarity (i.e., closeness) and to minimize conflict (i.e., separation). However, the dynamic balance of the family system is suddenly disrupted when Mr. Balasco and his father argue. After working many years on the farm and "barely surviving" on the income, Mr. Balasco decides to leave the farm. He recalls:

> I had an argument with my father. We had an agreement to split everything down the middle and I had a field of cabbage and he took that away from me . . . and I had a field of corn and he took that away from me . . . and I said, "Wait a minute" and he said, "If you don't like it here go."

Mr. Balasco's leavetaking marks a point at which he and his father are no longer able to complement each other within the realm of family interaction. Conflict between the two men occurs when Mr. Balasco's father intensifies his authoritarian behavioral stance and expects a corresponding submissive or powerless behavioral posture from his son. The extreme behaviors and expectations of Mr. Balasco's father threaten to terminate Mr. Balasco's participation in the dialogue entirely by forcing him into a situation in which he confronts the possibility of amplifying the behavioral posture associated with separation. The argument between the two men denotes family interaction at a stalemate. The resolution of the conflict—Mr. Balasco's departure from the farm—signals the triumph of movement over stagnation; Mr. Balasco chooses to move away from the family system rather than being forced into an increasingly stagnant role within it. Mr. Balasco recalls that his father was "despondent" over the separation. A recollection in which Mr. Balasco describes his father as visibly sad is extremely rare in the narrative and its occurrence here points to the impact which Mr. Balasco's departure has on the family.

By leaving the farm, Mr. Balasco finally appears to be making a choice that will benefit himself rather than his parents. However, his actions continue to serve the family system. Had Mr. Balasco decided to remain on the farm, the continuity of the family dialogue would have been seriously threatened by stagnation. Mr. Balasco's choice to leave allows the dialogue between himself and his parents to continue although on a qualitatively and structurally different level. He recalls:

> I used to go back to the farm and help on my days off and cut hay for them . . . we were happy then.

Mr. Balasco resumes his work on the farm for free and the conflict between Mr. Balasco and his father appears to be neutralized. However, he limits this "submissive" interaction with his parents to his "days off" from another job away from the farm. Mr. Balasco's contribution to the family dialogue has changed. He appears to have gained both spatial and relational distance from his parents. The system compensates for his loss by rebalancing its interactional expectations, thereby altering the family dialogue both qualitatively and structurally. However, although

Mr. Balasco seems to have achieved increased relational distance from his parents, his choice of job belies his reliance on an interactional context such as the one created in his family. Mr. Balasco goes to work for a local state mental "institution" in which the conceptual, volitional, and emotional expectations closely resemble those in his family. Thus, although Mr. Balasco manages a separation in space, his attainment of distance from his parents is still qualitatively limited.

The way in which Mr. Balasco handles interaction in the affective or emotional realm of family life further illustrates his tentative separation from the family. A review of the narrative reveals that in Mr. Balasco's family of origin, particular complementary interactions contribute to the family's dialogue in the emotional dimension. The primary motif associated with closeness is emotional stamina or the ability in interaction to refrain from showing or articulating feelings. The major theme linked to separation is emotional vulnerability or the tendency to display, express, and "give in to" affect. Members of the Balasco family minimize distance in the affective dimension by striving for complementarity of the behaviors derived from these contrasting themes. Family members with emotional stamina attempt to "carry on" for family members who are overwhelmed with feelings. Kantor (1975) notes that family members who neither share nor articulate their affect undermine the degree of separateness which they can attain from the family group. Thus, the predominant behavioral expectations around affect (i.e., those associated with closeness) in Mr. Balasco's family of origin serve to discourage the attainment of relational distance. Mr. Balasco's description of himself as an individual, who as a child and later as an adult, rarely revealed or shared feelings underscores his tentative separation from his family and, more specifically, his parents. The following interchange provides a nice illustration of Mr. Balasco's affective stance within the context of his family of origin. The narrative concerns his own and his family's reaction to the death of his mother.

Interviewer: When you found out, do you remember how you felt?

Mr. Balasco: I felt . . . I was working for a contractor . . . I didn't feel too well.

Interviewer: Did you feel sad or angry?

Mr. Balasco: I don't know whether I'm inhuman, I just didn't . . . it seemed like I went into a web. I just wasn't hurt . . . I accepted it. I think that I was probably one of the only ones in the family that accepted that . . . the other ones, they broke down . . . you know I hate to keep saying this about myself, but I'm a little different from the rest of them for the simple reason life goes on, the world doesn't end because you and I die.

Here Mr. Balasco's inability to experience and articulate affect limits the degree of individual separateness which he can achieve from the family. Notably, although Mr. Balasco insists that he accepts the loss, he displays none of the affects normally associated with grief. Mr. Balasco's willingness to meet behavioral expectations associated with closeness—demonstrating emotional stamina by "carrying on" for the emotionally weak and demonstrative members of his family—points to his continued commitment to the family dialogue long after he has moved away from the farm and his family. Paradoxically, although Mr. Balasco's behaviors function in the service of the family's distance minimization goal, his actions simultaneously isolate and alienate him from members of his family.

A closer look at Mr. Balasco's description of his parents and his relationship to them provides more specific information about the nature of the family's relational configuration and Mr. Balasco's position in it. Examples from the previous narrative suggest that, for Mr. Balasco, one parent plays a more dominant role than the other in striving for fulfillment of the family's distance minimization goal. Mr. Balasco's narrative indicates that he perceives his father as occupying this "dominant" position. Mr. Balasco consistently describes his father as assuming a behavioral posture connected to closeness, while he perceives his mother as behaving congruently with expectations associated with both closeness and separation. Mr. Balasco depicts his father as an authoritarian decision-maker who embodies emotional and physical stamina and who endeavors to perpetuate the family's ethnic and occupational identities. References to his father as powerless, unproductive, or physically or emotionally vulnerable are rare occurrences in his narrative. In contrast, such statements made by Mr. Balasco in reference to his mother are much more frequent. The following statement is illustrative:

> My mother was sick for about 20 years and she went to the Lahey Clinic and they told her if she would cut out using salts and eating fats, but she was brought up in this and she loved it and she would eat all of this stuff that she shouldn't have . . . she was told not to but she didn't want to change her life style. Portuguese people, you know, they like fats and she used to say, "If I'm going to die, let me eat what I want."

Although Mr. Balasco describes his mother as perpetuating the family's ethnic identity, he also focuses on her longstanding physical vulnerability. He sees her as a parent who assumes behavioral positions associated with both closeness and separation, respectively. References which Mr. Balasco makes to his mother as visibly "upset" when Robert leaves home and his recollection that she "cried over the sink" while working in the kitchen further illustrates this juxtapositioning of contrasting postures.

Notably, Mr. Balasco's references in the narrative stress identification in his relationship with his father and complementarity in his relationship with his mother. The following statements exemplify this point:

I'm not like the rest of them. I look like my father and act just like my father and my father acted just like me.

Now my mother, she was something. You could count on her if you needed help . . . she would always give you a dollar if you needed it.

In the first statement, Mr. Balasco seems to merge his own identity with the identity of his father. Here and in other excerpts from the data, Mr. Balasco appears to have substantial difficulty acknowledging personal or qualitative differences between himself and his father. Mr. Balasco's narrative is filled with examples in which he likens his behaviors to those of his father. In his comment above about his mother, Mr. Balasco recognizes behavioral complementarity. He depicts his mother as a reliable nurturant provider and refers to himself as in need of what she has to offer. Although Mr. Balasco perceives his behavioral posture as identical to that of his father and complementary to that of his mother, a careful examination of his narrative reveals that he both identifies with and complements the behavioral positions of each parent. The most striking example of behavior complementarity with his father is Mr. Balasco's willingness to work on the farm for free well into his adult life. Mr. Balasco's identification with his mother is evident as he shares her investment in farming and perpetuating the family's ethnic identity.

Thus, Mr. Balasco and his parents comprise a trio of family members who both identify with and complement one another's behavioral positions. However, Mr. Balasco's perception implies that he has difficulty recognizing a three-person system. Rather, he perceives two contrasting dyadic relationship structures. He depicts a father-son dyad held together by intense identification and a mother-son dyad sustained by behavioral complementarity. Mr. Balasco's perception appears to reflect his role in the family dialogue and his position within the family's relational configuration. Speculatively, it is Mr. Balasco's identification with his father's behavioral posture (i.e., behaviors associated with closeness) that allows Mr. Balasco to at times assume the behavioral posture associated with separation without risking amplification of this position. For example, Mr. Balasco's identification with the tough, authoritarian stance of his father permits Mr. Balasco to occasionally occupy a less powerful interactional role in the family without feeling so powerless that he is helpless to move out of that role. Thus, Mr. Balasco's part in the family dialogue is a changing one in which he is both capable of and expected to assume behavioral postures linked to both closeness and separation. Mr. Balasco's behavioral flexibility makes his contribution to the family dialogue an important one. Mr. Balasco's perception of familial relationships also illuminates his position in the relational configuration of the family. His intense identification with his father makes separation through opposition to behavioral expectations difficult and separation through amplification of behavioral expectations impossible. Thus, the degree of relational distance or separateness which Mr. Balasco can ultimately attain from either parent is limited. It is through this matrix of relationships and his perception of them that Mr. Balasco remains tied to the family and involved in the family dialogue. Thus, he plays an integral part in minimizing distance within his family of origin.

Mrs. Balasco: Family of Origin

Mrs. Balasco's description of her childhood and adolescence suggests that she, too, is a primary figure in the family dialogue and, consequently, occupies a special position in the relational configuration which constitutes the family system. As the narrative is reviewed, notable similarities appear between relational patterns in her family and those in the family of her husband.

Mrs. Balasco's recollections of her early childhood years are dominated by the presence of her mother. She repeatedly describes her mother as the family member who tended and cared for the young and the sick. From Mrs. Balasco's description, her mother appears to be the "dominant" parent, or the family member most involved in striving to meet the family's distance minimization goal. While Mrs. Balasco depicts her mother as assuming a behavioral stance associated with closeness, she perceives her father as behaving in a manner congruent with both closeness and separation. She recollects:

> . . . he didn't have time for us, he works split shifts . . . he worked funny hours . . . 'cause he would come home in the morning and go to work around four and then he would come home around nine and he had like split shifts and I don't know what he did during the day . . . my mother would fix lunch for him . . . and then he would go back to work and then a few hours later he would come home and then he would go back to work again and then he would come home around seven; but he was good with us . . . he would rock us and read us stories.

> . . . when the kids left I'm sure that it must have hurt my father very much but he didn't show it much . . . he was quiet . . .

Although Mrs. Balasco describes her father as "taking care of" the family financially, she recalls that he is often unable to offer the type of direct nurturing made available by her mother. In addition, Mrs. Balasco recollects her father as occasionally relying on others to have his needs met.

As Mrs. Balasco's perception of her relationship to both parents is examined, a configuration similar to that in her husband's family emerges. Mrs. Balasco's relationship with her mother appears based solely on identification and her relationship with her father seems grounded in behavioral complementarity. These examples from her narrative are illustrative:

> I guess I'm like my mother was . . . she was happy keeping the kids content . . . taking care of my sisters and brothers.

I've always had a lot of responsibility as far as children go, and I never resented it and I still don't.
I remember when my brother Jimmy was in the hospital, I had to take care of the kids that were at
home. And sometimes when my mother went to the hospital to visit him, I would take care of the
kids.

. . . my father . . . he really wasn't affectionate like my mother . . . well, he was warm, when we
were sick he had a lot of compassion.

Here, Mrs. Balasco is strongly identified with the behavioral posture of her
mother. Mrs. Balasco perceives herself as a primary caretaker in the family.
However, when describing her father, Mrs. Balasco acknowledges complementarity in their relationship and is able to recognize herself as one of the sick
children. Although Mrs. Balasco describes two contrasting dyadic relationship
structures, scrutiny of the material reveals that Mrs. Balasco both identifies with
and complements the behavioral posture of each parent. She shares nurturing
qualities with her father and as a sickly child (from birth on) complements the
caretaking behaviors of her mother. Mrs. Balasco's depiction of these relationships
suggests that she, like her husband, is unable to perceive the three-person system at
the heart of the relational configuration in her family. She opts rather for a view of
contrasting dyadic relationships based on identification and behavioral complementarity. As in her husband's case, Mrs. Balasco's perception reflects her role in
the family dialogue and her position in the matrix of systemic relationships. Mrs.
Balasco is adept at assuming contrasting behavioral postures and thus plays an
important role in sustaining the complementarity of the family's dialogue. Her
involvement in the dialogue limits the extent to which she can separate or achieve
relational distance from either parent.

In general, Mrs. Balasco remembers a "happy" and "contented" childhood.
Although the dialogue created around distance minimization is disrupted on
several occasions (i.e., the loss of Alan and Evelyn), the family system is able to
compensate and sustain behavioral complementarity by rebalancing existing systemic relationships. There are still other children for whom to care and family
members invested in caring for them. However, when Mrs. Balasco's mother
unexpectedly dies, the family system faces a major disruption of behavioral
complementarity. The family's loss of the primary caretaker interrupts the flow of
the dialogue and the system is literally "split up." For a week following the death,
the sick and the younger children in the family are sent to stay with relatives; the
behavioral demands made by these family members cannot be met in the system.
Ultimately, the family system attempts to compensate for the loss and restore
complementary interaction by making qualitative and structural changes in its
relational configuration. In short, the system strives to fill the position in the
dialogue left vacant by Mrs. Balasco's mother. As the narrative reveals, the
replacement is Mrs. Balasco. As she assumes the duties of her mother, family

members regroup and the dialogue is reconstructed. However, this new systemic balance is precarious as it depends on Mrs. Balasco's adaptation to a role in the dialogue in which she meets the parenting needs of the family at the expense of having her own needs adequately met. Mrs. Balasco's responsibilities in the family eventually interfere with her participation in normal adolescent activities. She recalls:

> I never went out with boys . . . I never experienced much of life outside the home.

> I had to drop out of high school . . . it was too much with the responsibilities of taking care of the kids and doing chores.

The already precarious balance of the relationship system is threatened further when Mrs. Balasco turns 17 and the family is evicted from their home of 21 years. She remembers:

> Well some new people bought the house and the tenants had to move out . . . and it was hard to find apartments with a lot of kids then . . . I wanted to get a job because we needed money then . . . my father didn't want me to get a job because he wanted me to stay home with the kids . . . . so I went to live with my friend who, like I told you, was like a second mother to me . . . and she had a little baby that I used to take care of . . .

Here, although Mrs. Balasco downplays any conflict between herself and her father, she is essentially describing a breakdown in the complementarity of the family dialogue—a point at which Mrs. Balasco and her father are no longer able to complement each other in the realm of family interaction. A crisis occurs in the system when Mrs. Balasco's father intensifies his authoritarian parental posture, anticipating a corresponding childlike submissive posture from his daughter. The position assumed by Mrs. Balasco's father threatens to terminate his daughter's role in the family dialogue entirely by forcing her into a situation in which she confronts the possibility of amplifying the behavioral stance associated with separation. However, Mrs. Balasco decides to move away from the family system rather than be forced into a stagnant role within it. Mrs. Balasco's departure disrupts the dialogue significantly, though, as the role of primary caretaker is vacated once more. The survival of the system is in question as Mrs. Balasco's father is unable to fill the vacated position adequately and the family becomes fragmented. Mrs. Balasco recalls:

> . . . he got a lady to take Gail in and Gail went and she lived with a lady that had two other children, and so my brother Kenny went to live with my father . . .

In retrospect, Mrs. Balasco's decision to leave home suggests that she has finally allowed her own needs rather than the needs of her family to dictate her actions. However, her decision ultimately serves the family system. Had she remained at home, the family dialogue would have been threatened by stagnation. Mrs. Balasco's choice to leave facilitates the continuation of the dialogue although on a qualitatively and structurally different level. A few years after her departure from the family, Mrs. Balasco leaves the home of her friend to get married "because Gail and Kenny still needed somebody." Thus, as she did eight years earlier, Mrs. Balasco replaces her mother at the expense of her own personal growth. Mrs. Balasco's comments about her marriage illustrate this point:

> The boy that I married was nice and everything like that . . . he wasn't fresh or wise or nothing like that . . . you know we lived together like a brother and sister . . . we didn't know nothing about sex and we were together a couple of years like that . . .

When she initally leaves home, Mrs. Balasco appears to have achieved increased relational distance from her family. However, her choices and actions in the years following her departure belie her ties to the system and her reliance on an interactional context such as the one created in her family. Mrs. Balasco's choice of living situation immediately after her departure from her family, her decision to marry, and her choice in later years of a job in which the volitional, emotional, and conceptual expectations resemble those in her family of origin all point to the limited relational distance which she is able to attain.

The nature of Mrs. Balasco's involvement in the family dialogue is also evident in the affective dimension of the family's experience. A review of the narrative reveals that, in Mrs. Balasco's family of origin, there are particular interactional expectations or rules connected to affect. As in the other experiential fields, there are expectations associated with closeness and expectations associated with separation. The expectations or rules created around closeness include emotional adequacy and endurance, or the ability to bear affect without sharing or articulating it. Among the behavioral expectations associated with separation are emotional vulnerability and the display and expression of affect. Generally in her narrative, Mrs. Balasco is depicted as an emotional isolate who never shares or expresses feelings in the presence of other members of her family of origin. Earlier in the narrative, she stresses the fact (while crying copiously) that she does not know how her siblings or her father feel about her mother's death. The following comments further substantiate the atmosphere of emotional isolation in her family and hint at her role as the bearer of affect:

Interviewer: Did you talk about it at the time in terms of helping each other. . .sharing your feelings together?

Mrs. Balasco: No. I think we just all kept our feelings to ourselves.

Interviewer: And your father?

Mrs. Balasco: No, my father never talked very much about it . . . he was a very quiet man.

Interviewer: How did you deal with it?

Mrs. Balasco: I kept it to myself, but it really bothered me a lot.

       . . . I don't know, they may feel the same way, but I don't talk to them about it because I know that I always cry.

       . . . you'd think after 30 years it wouldn't bother me no more.

Although burdened with feelings, Mrs. Balasco refrains from sharing knowledge about an affect-laden event with other members of her family of origin and thus appears to bear the affect for the system. The fact that Mrs. Balasco maintains this position 30 years after the event and appears to bear a disproportionate amount of sadness suggests her continued involvement in the dialogue of her family of origin. Paradoxically, although Mrs. Balasco's intends her behavioral stance to insure closeness among members of her family of origin, her actions ultimately result in an experience of emotional isolation for her.

Comparative Summary: The Balascos' Families of Origin

In overview, the relational patterns described by the Balascos in their respective families of origin are remarkably similar. Both families are highly invested in minimizing familial distance and members of each family approach the task by participating in a dialogue or a set of complementary interactions derived from themes specific to their family system. The sensitivity of the respective families to increases in intrafamilial distance makes the negotiation of the task of adolescent separation difficult and often the only distancing options available to separating family members are relatively extreme ones. However, the fact that these "adolescent" separations are both anticipated and initiated by both the parents and the adolescent children suggests that these particular children play a peripheral part in the family dialogue. Although the leavetakings of these adolescents produce shifts in the dynamic balance of the system, these shifts are not major and do not require substantial qualitative or structural systemic compensation. These children, through their separation, are able to attain some degree of physical and relational distance from their families.

    In contrast, the unexpected and untimely separations due to institutionalization or death which occur in each family appear to constitute a relatively more serious threat to system survival. In these instances, the system may move into a state of major imbalance or crisis in which the complementarity of the dialogue is seriously threatened or even totally disrupted. Both families discussed in the narrative compensate for such states of crisis by initiating changes in the structural and qualitative characteristics of the system. The loss of Mrs. Balasco's mother is the most striking example in the data of disruption in the family dialogue, ensuing systemic crisis and subsequent qualitative and structural compensation. Overall, members of both Mr. and Mrs. Balasco's families of origin appear to be involved to varying degrees in the minimization of familial distance and seem to contribute correspondingly to the family dialogue.

An examination of the data suggests that both Mr. and Mrs. Balasco play primary roles in minimizing distance in their respective families. The Balascos' perceptions of their relationships with their respective parents reflect both their role in the family dialogue (i.e., the behavioral postures which they assume) and their position in the relational configuration which constitutes the family system (i.e., the family members with whom the Balascos are most involved). Although each of the Balascos both identify with and complement the behavior of each of their parents, they are unable to perceive this experience. Rather, the Balascos describe two contrasting dyadic relationship structures based on identification and complementarity, respectively. Both Mr. and Mrs. Balasco describe themselves as strongly identified with the "dominant" parent and as involved in a complementary relationship with the other parent. The identification stressed by both Balascos appears to facilitate a shifting role in the family dialogue in which each is able to assume behavioral postures associated with both closeness and separation. In addition, the identification delays and undermines the degree of separateness which the Balascos can attain from their respective parents. When the Balascos do leave their families, the separations are qualitatively limited.

Speculatively, the ability of each of the Balascos and his or her parents to sustain complementary interaction, or the family dialogue, determines the extent of system stability. In each family, members appear to rely on this three-person system to compensate for qualitative and/or structural changes. The degree of success with which these three-person systems minimize distance varies and depends on the number and severity of systemic crises.

As the discussion shifts its focus to an exploration of relationships in the current Balasco family, the similarity of relational patterns is notable.

The Balascos' Current Family

Mr. and Mrs. Balasco meet and court while they are both employed at a local state mental institution; he is working as an aid on one of the hospital wards and she has a job as a cook in the kitchen. As Mr. Balasco works for an "institution" which respects authority and demands physical and emotional stamina, he is in a position which involves him in a dialogue similar to the one in his family of origin. Mrs. Balasco is employed as a cook and is directly involved in feeding and nurturing the sick. Her job provides her with the opportunity to contribute to an interactional context similar to the one in her family of origin. As they court and marry, the Balascos create a new dialogue that is both composed of the themes and behavioral rules which constituted interaction in their respective family systems and, at the same time, is a new entity or a synthesis of these elements. This new marital dialogue appears to be sustained in much the same way that the family dialogue was perpetuated in the Balascos' families of origin. That is, both the Balascos' perception of martial interaction, as well as the interaction itself, contribute to the functioning of the marital system.

As the Balascos talk about married life, both describe themselves as assuming behavioral postures which stem from their respective families of origin. Specifically, the Balascos relate behaviors which are associated with closeness and are similar to those of the "dominant" parent in their original families. Mr. Balasco prides himself on his ability to make things grow and to work on the land. Mrs. Balasco emphasizes her interest in nurturing activities such as creating a home and having children. As the Balascos discuss their shared goals at the time of marriage, this point is illustrated:

Interviewer: What would you say your shared goals were when you married? What did you want for yourselves?

Mr. Balasco: What I wanted was a house . . . see I never really wanted a house . . . I never really did . . . I always figures pay the rent, but Marie in fact, 'til this day any house that we got she has always been the constructor, the contractor. I'm an outside man. I hate wood with a passion. I'm a dirt man. It's all Marie's work that you see here, even the design of this house which I pay a lot of compliment to because you sit down and a house is a house but she has a lot of characteristics that go along with this.

Interviewer: So Mrs. Balasco, it sounds like you wanted to buy a house while your husband was content to just pay the rent.

Mrs. Balasco: Well, no. We bought the first house together.

Mr. Balasco: Well, but you were the one who went out and bought the house. I didn't go with her . . . she was the one who went out with all these real estate people.

Interviewer: Did you feel that you wanted the house?

Mr. Balasco: Yeah, we talked about it and after we got the house . . . after we knew that we were going to get it, I kind of did a lot of landscaping work 'cause the place didn't have no landscaping until I got there.

Interviewer: What other things did you want for yourselves as a couple?

Mr. Balasco: Well, we wanted children. I wasn't all washed up at age 25 or whatever age I was. Well, Marie more or less wanted it.

Thus, in their marital relationship, the Balascos appear to perpetuate behaviors and interests which reflect their strong identification with the "dominant" parent in their respective families. In addition, the Balascos' descriptions of one another closely resemble their descriptions of the other parent in their original families. The Balascos portray one another as assuming behavioral postures associated with both closeness and separation. Mrs. Balasco characterizes her husband in a way that is reminiscent of earlier comments about her father:

> . . . he's a hard worker, he's good to me and he's kind in a lot of ways . . . he's straight forward and honest and he certainly is a giving person . . . he doesn't feel as deep as I do . . . he keeps his feelings to himself . . . but he likes to talk, he likes to be the center of attention, and sometimes he's domineering . . .

To the extent that Mr. Balasco is a hard worker and is a giving and caring individual, he behaves congruently with expectations associated with closeness in Mrs. Balasco's family of origin. However, his tendency to be a quiet man who does not "feel . . . deep" (i.e., bear affect) sees Mr. Balasco assuming a behavioral posture linked to separation in his wife's family of origin. Mr. Balasco's description of his wife is quite reminiscent of his earlier comments about his mother. He notes:

> Marie is easy-going . . . and myself I'm what you would call a tight bastard . . . she is neat and clean and artistic. When I was going with Marie whatever I wanted to do she fit right in . . . she takes care of the kids when they're sick . . . she works hard in the house.

Mr. Balasco's likening of his wife to his mother is most striking in the affective realm. Earlier in chapter 4, Mr. Balasco recalls his wife "crying over the stove" in much the same way that he recalls his mother "crying over the sink." To the extent that Mrs. Balasco fits in, works hard, and takes care of the children, she meets behavioral expectations associated with closeness in Mr. Balasco's family of origin. Mrs. Balasco's expression of affect and displays of emotional vulnerability see her assuming a behavioral posture connected to separation in her husband's original family. In summary, it is likely that the Balascos' perception of themselves as predominantly assuming behavioral postures associated with closeness allows them to exercise a degree of flexibility in assuming postures linked with both closeness and separation. In this way, the marital dialogue sustains complementarity, and the Balascos begin to pursue the goal of distance minimization within their marriage. A look at the spouse system before the birth of the children confirms the mutuality of the goal:

Interviewer: It seems that one of the unspoken rules was that you always did everything together?

Mrs. Balasco: Well, yes . . . well not always. I mean I could go to the movies with a friend.

Mr. Balasco: Sure.

Mrs. Balasco: It wasn't that I couldn't go out if Ben wanted to go out with a friend, but it was a rare occurrence.

Mr. Balasco: We were like two peas in a pod.

During the early years of their marriage and after the birth of their first child, Christine, the Balascos appear able to sustain a stable systemic dialogue. However, prior to the birth of the second child, the continuity of family interaction is threatened by a number of events. At this time, Mrs. Balasco begins to experience gynecological problems. She suffers two miscarriages and finally gives birth to a second child, Teddy. Subsequently, Mrs. Balasco is made aware of the seriousness of a long-standing blood condition (later diagnosed as pernicious anemia) and is strongly advised by her doctors to have a hysterectomy. She ignores this advice and becomes pregnant with a third child, Davy. Five years after Davy's birth, Mrs. Balasco allows a hysterectomy to be performed at the insistence of her doctors. In order to understand the impact of these events on the development of the family dialogue, it is necessary to reconstruct the configuration of relationships in the Balasco family before any of the children reach adolescence.

Generally, as Mrs. Balasco speaks of her children, she acknowledges her strong investment in minimizing intrafamilial distance. She admits:

> I don't know, maybe because I've been through so much maybe this is why . . . well I won't say that I overprotect the kids. I do want them to have a normal life . . . but maybe I'm a little bit more protective than I would be if I hadn't been through a lot of turmoil . . . if my life was a lot freer, maybe their life would be too.

Mrs. Balasco's apparent difficulty tolerating relational distance in contrast to her husband suggests that she may be the "dominant" parent in the current Balasco family. As the Balascos talk about their children, Mrs. Balasco is notably more involved in the task and primarily focuses her narrative on Davy. Her description of the other two children, Christine and Teddy, most often is embedded in her portrayal of her youngest son. Both parents agree that Mrs. Balasco developed a closer relationship with Davy over the years than did her husband. These comments are illustrative:

Mrs. Balasco: . . . well, I suppose in all fairness I have to say that I was closer to Davy . . . I probably was closer to Davy but it wasn't done with realization that this is my last child and I'm going to devote all my attention . . . it wasn't done . . . I had no other choice . . . I mean it was between him (Mr. Balasco) and me and he worked all day so I was there . . . wherever I went, Davy went.

Mr. Balasco: Davy was a sick kid . . . I went to work and Ma seemed to get closer.

As she speaks about Davy, Mrs. Balasco's tone is almost apologetic:

> What do you do with a little one that has a problem like that . . . you just try to make him a complete person and that's very hard to do, and of course in making him into a complete person you spend a lot of time with him and you can't let a baby stay in bed without talking to him and playing with him. He really had no activity outside . . . he wasn't like Teddy who I could get dressed and let him play out back in the sand box . . . so I would arrange these diversions . . . painting, drawing, and stories.

Mrs. Balasco's recollections of Davy and Teddy imply that from early on the amount of relational distance between mother and each son differed significantly. Additional comments made by Mrs. Balasco lend support to this point:

> Had Davy been able to do the types of things that Teddy was able to do I think then I could say to myself, well maybe I did this because I favored one more than the other . . . then I could see where you could make a comparison because their ages were close and I had devoted all this attention to Davy and he was well and healthy. I would really feel guilty that I did this but because of the situation at the time, I honestly say that I don't feel guilty. I feel bad that maybe Davy feels that I took over his life . . . I do feel badly in that respect, but it wasn't done with the intent that he was a well healthy child and I held him back and let Teddy go. When I think about Davy, I'm not ashamed, but I don't feel guilty about the care I've given him . . . but a lot of things I really feel that Davy missed out on. Like Christine went to dancing school and Teddy went to camp . . . Davy did neither of those two things. They both went to kindergarten and Davy didn't do that . . . when Davy was younger, I was home $\frac{9}{10}$ths of the time . . . Teddy is an outgoing person and he's always had a lot of friends and Davy never did but he was very contented within himself or seemed to be contented.

Both parents concur that while Davy was close to Mrs. Balasco, Teddy was close to his father. Mrs. Balasco states, "I think that Ben was a lot closer to Teddy." Mr. Balasco agrees, explaining:

> I was always closer to Teddy because you know why because I realize that Davy was a sick kid and I let him stay home and get better and I depended on, I drove the heaviness on to Ted. Not disliking either of them, but you know when your hand is bad you use the other hand. Teddy could be out in the truck with me.

While Mrs. Balasco's narrative depicts her as intensely focused on and overly close to Davy, Mr. Balasco's comments convey a sense of disconnectedness between himself and his youngest son. As Mr. Balasco talks about his children, his words seem to exclude Davy:

> I liked Christine . . . she was a real toughy girl . . . a spitfire, but in the Balasco family, there's very few boys, all girls, and I'm fortunate because I've got two boys and Teddy is a dead ringer for the Balasco side of the family . . . of the two boys, he's the only true looking Balasco.

Although he characterizes his daughter, Mr. Balasco's statement here is most directly concerned with his son Teddy. Described by both parents as an aggressive and tough youngster, Teddy possesses qualities of physical and emotional stamina that identify him with his father. Mr. Balasco's identification with Teddy is reminiscent of his identification with his father. In both instances Mr. Balasco stresses physical and behavioral resemblances. Mr. Balasco appears to experience some difficulty in acknowledging personal differences or relational distance between Teddy and himself. Both Mrs. Balasco's descriptive allusions to and comments about Christine ("When I was sick and out of the house, sometimes Christine would take over for me . . . take care of the kids . . . she was mature") and the comments made by her husband suggest that each parent felt relatively close to their daughter and perceived her as similar to themselves in many ways. Christine is portrayed as possessing the emotional and physical stamina of her father and the nurturant, caretaking qualities of her mother. Thus, identification is perceived as the basis for Christine's relationship with each parent.

As the narrative illustrates, Davy's relationships with his parents differ considerably from those of his siblings. Overall, Davy seems, on the one hand, to have the closest relationship with his mother than any of his siblings and, on the other hand, to have the most distant relationship with his father than the rest of his siblings. Within physical space alone, there is a marked difference in the Balascos' relationship to Davy as compared to the other two children. Davy's need to remain in bed and at home places him in close proximity to his mother who keeps him occupied in his room while sending the other children out to play. In the evenings, at home from work, Mr. Balasco is more likely to spend time with his two healthy children than to venture into Davy's room to visit. As the children grow, the situation remains the same and a particular relational configuration begins to typify the Balasco family system. When Christine and Teddy leave to go to kindergarten, camp or dancing school, Davy stays at home. As Christine and Teddy increase relational distance between themselves and the family by seeking friends in the neighborhood, Davy remains in the house, a constant companion to his mother and an increasing stranger to his father. As a temporarily disabled child, Davy is less capable of identifying with the parental qualities (i.e., caretaking, physical and emotional stamina) which cement the relationships between his mother, father, and siblings. Rather, Davy's illness and physical fragility place him in a complementary relationship with each of his parents in which he assumes the behavioral postures linked to separation in their respect for families of origin. As a sick child, Davy complements his mother's caretaking posture and, thus, at an early age becomes her most frequent partner in sustaining a significant part of the Balascos' family dialogue. As a physically fragile child who is unable to provide for himself, Davy complements his father's physical stamina and ability to carry on and provide for others ("I thought I was doing my share by bringing home the bacon"). However, Mr. Balasco's absence from the home makes it difficult for him to engage closely in a dialogue with Davy, and as Davy and Mrs. Balasco grow closer within the domain of the home. Mr. Balasco notably becomes more of "an outside man."

To summarize, prior to the adolescence of the Balasco children, a specific configuration of relationships has emerged in the family. Both of the Balascos appear moderately involved with their daughter Christine in relationships based on identification. While both parents are engaged with Teddy, Mr. Balasco emerges as the closer parent of the two. His relationship with Teddy also seems to stress identification. In contrast to his siblings, Davy's relationships with both parents are based on complementarity rather than identification. In addition, the complementarity is largely fixed rather than flexible. That is, each of the relating partners generates the same, or similar behavioral postures in the relationship time after time. Although Davy complements the behavioral stance of both parents, he is much more intensely engaged with his mother in sustaining a dialogue and thereby minimizing distance in the family system. Notably, although Davy meets behavioral expectations associated with separation, he never amplifies his posture to a point at which stagnation becomes a threat. Therefore, Davy is able to continue to contribute to the family dialogue and the dynamic balance of the system remains relatively stable. With this configuration of relationships in mind, the discussion will return to focus on the events of loss which threatened the Balasco family prior to Davy's birth.

To review briefly, Mrs. Balasco suffered two miscarriages before she gave birth to her second child, Teddy. After his birth, she learned of the seriousness of her blood condition and was told by doctors that conceiving another child could pose a threat to her life. Mrs. Balasco was advised to have a hysterectomy. She ignored this advice and conceived and gave birth to her third child, Davy. Five years later, she consented to a hysterectomy. In the following interchange, the Balascos recall the events preceding Davy's birth:

Interviewer: How did you feel about the consideration of a hysterectomy . . . did you want to have more children?

Mr. Balasco: No, I didn't. No, I thought we ought to stop there while we were ahead. But luck was Davy came along.

Interviewer: Luck? Was Davy unplanned?

Mr. Balasco: Yeah, we kind of unplanned that one . . . in fact none of my kids were really planned.

Mrs. Balasco: Well we never did anything to prevent them.

Interviewer: Were you concerned about your wife at that point?

Mr. Balasco: Yeah, I was worried about her . . . and if I was ever left with two small little kids and a big house . . .

Mrs. Balasco: It was a chance and I knew it too.

Interviewer: So, this was a disagreement between the two of you?

Mr. Balasco: No.

Mrs. Balasco: No, not really. As far as open disagreement, no. I was happy that I was pregnant again and I was happy that it was terminated in the birth of the baby.

Interviewer: But the two of you did seem to have different feelings about the hysterectomy.

Mr. Balasco: That's right . . . but I always figure if that's what you need then go in and do it. Of course, nobody likes to go into the hospital.

Interviewer: But you didn't argue about this?

Mr. Balasco: No. That was the least of our worries. No arguments about that.

Interviewer: (to Mrs. Balasco) It sounds though, that a decision about a hysterectomy was kind of a big thing in your life.

Mrs. Balasco: Yes it was.

Mr. Balasco: She was kind of set to make more life and I wanted it to end.

Interviewer: And yet, it didn't cause any discussion?

Mr. Balasco: No, I can't recall.

What is noteworthy in this exchange about a relatively anxiety-filled time for the Balasco family is the absence of references to marital conflict. Although the system stands to permanently lose a crucial family member (i.e., Mrs. Balasco), the couple seems unable to initiate action either as a unit or individually to insure Mrs. Balasco's survival. However, given the reluctance of the Balascos to directly share feelings, particularly feelings about separation, with one another, their denial of conflict is congruent with the emotionally isolated stance of each. In their narrative, the Balascos convey a picture of system stability; however, close scrutiny of the material reveals that the marital dialogue is, in fact, threatened by disruption and the system is experiencing a constant state of crisis until after Davy's birth. As illustrated earlier, the stability of the marital dialogue is based on the ability of the Balascos to perceive themselves as assuming behavioral postures associated with closeness. Mr. Balasco conceives of himself as an individual who works hard, perpetuates his family ethnic identity, helps things grow, and demonstrates emotional and physical stamina. Mrs. Balasco views herself as a nurturant caretaker figure who tends the home and the children. Although each of the Balascos assume behavioral postures associated with both closeness and separation during the course of the marital relationship, they are highly invested in not acknowledging the occasions upon which they behave in a manner congruent with separation. The marital dialogue is threatened during the time period under consideration because each of the Balascos must confront the fact that he or she is meeting behavioral expectations linked to separation. This process begins when Mrs. Balasco learns of the seriousness of her illness. Here she is forced to acknowledge that she is a "sick" woman. In the past, particularly as a sick child, Mrs. Balasco struggled against amplification of this posture by identifying herself with the caretaking and nurturant qualities of her mother. Thus, in the present context, a hysterectomy represents not a life saving measure but an obstacle which terminates the potential for further mothering activities. As Mrs. Balasco refuses to make the decision regarding surgery herself, the most likely person to persuade her would be her husband. However, although he admits that he and his wife thought differently about the matter, and that he was concerned about her, Mr. Balasco seems powerless to act. His stated dislike of hospitals ("he has . . . a block about sickness or anything to do with hospitals or doctors") referred to earlier in the narrative appears responsible for his inability to mobilize himself in the situation. If Mr. Balasco chooses to assume responsibility for his wife and force her to enter a hospital for surgery, he must confront separation and the possibility of ultimate loss. If he remains passive in the situation, Mr. Balasco may similarly be forced to confront separation and loss in the event that his wife's health deteriorates and she dies. Thus, he is bound in an increasingly powerless position in which either passivity or activity necessitates a confrontation with separation and loss. An amplification of Mr. Balasco's feelings of powerlessness threatens to make his role in the marital dialogue a stagnant one. As exemplified in his relationship with his father, Mr. Balasco is able to tolerate the experience of powerlessness only to a point after which he struggles to regain a more powerful position. Within the marital relationship, Mr. Balasco fights to avoid amplification of the behavioral posture and struggles to sustain the flow of the marital dialogue by impregnating his wife with the "unplanned" child, Davy. Here, Mr. Balasco assumes a behavioral stance associated with closeness when he literally plants a seed.

This shift in Mr. Balasco's position in the marital dialogue results in a corresponding change in the role of his wife. Within the context of pregnancy, the danger to her health increases and once more, she runs the risk of amplifying a behavioral posture associated with separation. This on-going crisis in the marital dialogue appears to come to an end when Mrs. Balasco delivers Davy. The following interchange is illustrative:

Interviewer: And then after Davy was born did you have a hysterectomy?

Mrs. Balasco: No, I didn't have a hysterectomy until five years afterwards.

Interviewer: Was it a big decision at that point?

Mrs. Balasco: Yes it was.

Interviewer: How did the two of you feel about it?

Mr. Balasco: I never got into that one.

Mrs. Balasco: I really didn't want it. I don't know why . . . and I had been hospitalized for a number of different things and I guess that I had had a lot of sadness in my life and perhaps that was one of the reasons that I kept holding back. But it just came to a point that there was no choice and the choice was made for me by the doctors.

Interviewer: (to Mr. Balasco) And you knew about this?

Mr. Balasco: I knew about it but I didn't get involved in it. I figured that she knew how sick she was and if the doctor said that is what you should have . . . I do not rule over her.

Mrs. Balasco: I don't think that I realized at the time how sick I was. You know you get to a point in sickness that you can't understand yourself . . . you can't rationalize with it.

Interviewer: So even though you knew that this was really going to affect her health you stayed out?

Mr. Balasco: That's right.

These comments suggest that the threat to the marital dialogue has diminished significantly. Here the Balascos both deny generating behaviors associated with separation. Mr. Balasco avoids feelings of powerlessness by remaining uninvolved in his wife's dilemma, and Mrs. Balasco continues to deny the seriousness of her physical condition. What is unspoken in this interchange, but has already been illustrated in other excerpts from the data, is the manner in which the Balascos intensify their occupation of behavioral positions associated with closeness after Davy's birth. His birth appears to facilitate this process which, in turn, allows the Balascos once more to perceive themselves as meeting behavioral expectations linked to closeness. Consequently the marital dialogue is stabilized. Careful examination suggests that it is Davy's presence which sustains the dialogue. Notably, the Balascos intensify behaviors associated with closeness in relation to Davy who as a sickly child generates behaviors associated with separation. Thus, a new relational configuration is created in the family in which Davy, rather than his siblings, plays a major role in the perpetuation of the family dialogue and the minimization of intrafamilial distance.

The Balascos' Current Family: Negotiating Adolescence

As the discussion shifts to an exploration of the manner in which the Balasco family negotiates the developmental task of adolescence, some familiar relational patterns appear. At the age of 18, Christine decides to marry after her high school graduation. According to Davy, Christine actually elopes while the family is vacationing and is then forced back home by her parents to stage a fake wedding for the family. Mr. and Mrs. Balasco do not mention an "elopement" in their narratives, but they do express ambivalent feelings about Christine's decision to marry. Mrs. Balasce explains that she would have liked Christine to further her education before marrying. Mr. Balasco asserts that he wished the couple had waited until they made more money. If Christine did indeed elope, her actions would be reminiscent of the abrupt leavetakings that characterized some of the adolescent separations in the Balascos' families of origin. However, the evidence of an elopement is not substantiated by Mr. and Mrs. Balasco. What is evident, however, is the fact that both the Balascos and their daughter were able to allow the separation. The system's collaboration around the separation suggests that Christine's role in the family dialogue was not crucial. As she leaves, Christine challenges conceptual and volitional rules which contribute to family interaction. Both parents most often describe Christine, of the three children, as a substitute caretaker when Mrs. Balasco is away from the home. Christine's departure and marriage limits the extent to which she can continue to assume this position.

The Balascos seem to have more difficulty negotiating the developmental task of adolescence with their eldest son, Teddy. As Teddy approaches the age of 17, he begins to skip school. Mr. Balasco comments:

> Teddy has been unhappy since the move. He's been skipping school. I can't understand Teddy's part of it. In about three months from now when he gets the . . . that license, he'll be able to take the goddamn truck and go where he pleases. I can't understand the logic of it. We are turning over this $5,000 piece of equipment and saying here you have your license now you can come and go.

As the potential for separation between Teddy and his parents increases, Teddy begins to challenge the family's behavioral expectations. Specifically, he challenges the expectations of the parent with whom he is closer, his father. By skipping school, Teddy opposes the family rule that the oldest boy receive an education. In addition, Teddy, who had previously been actively involved in a small plowing operation with his father expresses reluctance to take over the business. Mr. Balasco comments on this turn of events:

Interviewer: Teddy doesn't want to do it?

Mr. Balasco: Well, I'll have to say, "Ted, must I let this go?"

Interviewer: So you would push him a little bit, you would like him to do it?

Mr. Balasco: Yeah. I don't want to lose this business. When I want to let go, I will. Until then, I'm the boss.

Teddy's reluctance to assume responsibility for the business is a challenge to his father's expectations in both the conceptual and volitional dimensions of the family's experience. Teddy defies expectations that he perpetuate the family's occupational identity, and he defies the authoritarian stance of his father. Both the fact that Teddy initiates oppositional moves earlier than his sister and that these moves seem to have more of an impact on the system suggest that Teddy's contribution to the family dialogue is significantly greater than that of his sister. Correspondingly, the Balascos seem to have a more difficult time negotiating separation with their eldest son than they did with their daughter. The relatively extreme moves which Teddy makes towards separation imply that the options for increasing relational distance between himself and his parents, particularly his father, are limited. Mr. Balasco's rigid stance regarding the family business is reminiscent of his father's no-negotiation approach to the children's participation in farm work.

In order to understand the family system's response to Davy's encounter with adolescence, it is necessary to examine his perception of his parents, his description of his relationship with each of them, and his perception of himself. In addition, it is important to review the manner in which the Balascos perceive Davy as he makes the transition from childhood to adolescence. Davy's description of his parents confirms points made earlier in the discussion about the quality and structure of relationships in the Balasco family. Notably, Davy's references to his mother dominate his narrative, while allusions to his father are substantially less frequent. Davy describes his mother in the the following way:

> . . . my mother is domineering . . . she tries too hard to run my life . . . she tries to tell me who my friends should be and where I should go . . . she snoops . . . she goes into my things . . . I had a log right, and after I found out that she had been reading it I threw it in the fire.

Here, Davy's perception of his mother as overprotective and interfering suggests that the behavioral complementarity which characterized Davy's relationship with his mother earlier in his life is breaking down. Although Davy is no longer a sick child, Mrs. Balasco continues to act in the intensified role of caretaker. Davy's portrayal of his mother implies that she is dangerously near to amplifying a behavioral posture associated with closeness. Davy describes his father as:

> . . . always by himself . . . he never goes anywhere . . . when my mother was in the hospital, my father didn't have time to clean, he was at work . . . I like my father but I don't know what I like about him.

Davy's portrayal of his father is notably vague. This vagueness suggests that Davy feels distant from his father, that he doesn't know him well. Their relationship is a disconnected one and seems to recapitulate the relationship between Davy and his father alluded to earlier in the discussion. To the extent that he describes his mother as involved in caretaking activities and his father as working, Davy perceives both parents as assuming behavioral postures connected to closeness. However, while Mrs. Balasco's behavioral position seems to directly influence and effect Davy, Mr. Balasco's stance has relatively little impact on him. These observations substantiate the fact that it is his mother with whom Davy is most involved in the family dialogue.

As Davy talks about himself, his role in the family dialogue and his position in the relational configuration of the family system are illuminated. In a manner reminiscent of his mother, Davy has difficulty recalling his childhood disability. He struggles to remember:

> I don't know. It's weird, because I can't hardly remember anything about being in a wheelchair . . . it's all blacked out.

Here, Davy fights to block out memories of himself as a disabled child who occupied a behavioral position associated with separation in the family. Mrs.

Balasco blocks out her memories of sickness as a child by recalling her identification with the nurturant caretaking qualities of her mother. Thus she avoids amplification of a behavioral posture associated with separation by striving to meet behavioral expectations associated with closeness. Notably both sets of behaviors stem from the family's dialogue. Davy's approach to a similar situation is significantly different from that of his mother. Although he seems to attempt to avoid amplification of the behavioral posture linked to separation, Davy has difficulty identifying with the postures antithetical to separation in either the dialogue of his mother or his father. In his narrative, Davy expresses concern about nurturance and caretaking; however, references to himself as involved in these activities are rare. Similarly in his dialogue with Mr. Balasco, Davy is cognizant of alternative postures but is unable to identify himself with them. When asked about his strengths and weaknesses, Davy responds, "I'm not as strong as I should be . . . muscles . . ." Here Davy recognizes one of the qualities (i.e., physical stamina) associated with closeness in his dialogue with his father, but seems unable to incorporate it into his perception of himself. Thus, Davy is in a position of struggling to avoid amplification of behaviors associated with separation while having an inadequate repertoire of contrasting or replacement behaviors. Davy's replacement behaviors are characterized by a superficial quality and are notably not derived from the behavioral dialogues in the Balasco family. These comments are illustrative:

> Like I see some 14-year-olders . . . and I call them immature, but then I have to remember that I'm only 14 . . . everyone my age are jerks, they're all immature little brats. That's why I hate talking about ages. I can't stand it. It bothers me . . . I hang around with kids older than me . . . some are in their twenties.

Here and in other excerpts from his narrative, Davy disqualifies the value of forming relationships with youngsters his age and stresses his desire to befriend older people. He seems to believe that association with older people will undercut the intensity with which he still meets behavioral expectations associated with separation in his family.

Davy's adolescent struggle with identity is reflected in the observations of his parents. Mrs. Balasco makes the following comments about Davy as an adolescent:

> . . . I think that he wants to get out of this cocoon he's in and I think that he wants to spread his wings and he's spreading them in a way that maybe a nine-or ten-year-old would do not knowing where to fly. And I think that in some respects, Davy is willing to get into a group whether it's right or wrong or indifferent as long as they accept him and yet I feel bad because I think that he certainly is smart enough to know right from wrong, but I don't think that he is applying good methods to his behavior. Yet, as long as they say come with us . . . he'll go.

I'm so close with Davy that I think that Davy feels like I'm trying to live his life . . . that, you know, really isn't so, but I can imagine why he would feel that way because we are, we were, close when he was younger, but I'm wondering if in trying to branch away from me that he needed some masculine identity, like with his father . . . He needed to move away from doing everything that momma . . .wants me to do . . . .

. . . I don't think that Davy could be a worker like Ben, a physically hard worker. I don't think that he could have the capacity.

In her comments, Mrs. Balasco seems to recognize Davy's need to grow and to oppose or challenge his childhood role in the family; however, her statements suggest that she still perceives her son as primarily assuming a behavioral posture associated with separation in the family dialogue. Mrs. Balasco portrays Davy as immature, as using poor judgment, as physically and emotionally inadequate, and as overly involved with her.

Mr. Balasco's observations of Davy are in the same vein as those of his wife. He comments:

Davy was a beautiful boy, but he got sick and when he'd get sick the whole family would feel that he needed help and they would give it to him . . . everything that they could. And this is what I think happened to him . . . I thought he was sick all the time and then when he got over it I depended more on Theodore . . . Davy isn't quite as strong as Theodore and I'll use Teddy to go with me and this and that . . . not that I don't love him (Davy), but a sick kid is a sick kid.

. . . I'd like Teddy to take over the business and use the money to get a college education . . . Davy, I would like to see him do what he wants to do . . . it makes no difference to me.

Although he seems to recognize the fact that Davy is no longer a "sick" child, Mr. Balasco ultimately depicts his son as occupying a behavioral position associated with separation in family interaction. Mr. Balasco continues to perceive Davy as sick and physically inadequate. In addition, his comments reflect his lack of involvement with Davy and his paucity of knowledge about his son's activities and interests apart from the family.

Thus, although Davy's behavioral posture has objectively changed (i.e., he is no longer a sick child), his parents continue to behave towards him as if he were still disabled. Mrs. Balasco remains overly-involved and protective towards her son, while Mr. Balasco stays distant and detached. Both parents attempt to maintain the fixed behavioral complementarity that characterized their respective relationships with Davy earlier in his life. As a result, Davy frequently finds himself in a position which forces him to meet behavioral expectations associated with separation without having the opportunity to learn behaviors associated with closeness in the family.

As Davy and his parents face the developmental task of adolescence, the family dialogue and the dynamic balance of the system are increasingly threatened. Davy, his mother, and his father are not prepared to negotiate a separation. Davy does not have a repertoire of behaviors that will help him successfully challenge parental expectations. Mr. and Mrs. Balasco are involved in relatively fixed dialogues with Davy which provide little room for movement or increased relational distance between partners. As Davy attempts to separate from his parents, he amplifies complementary family interaction, and stagnation threatens the family dialogue. Davy's first leavetaking from home at the age of 14 illustrates this process. Several months prior to the family's move, Davy, who had always been "a loner" began to make friends and establish himself within the context of a peer group. This was a major change for a youngster whose primary relational context had been within the home. Davy's parents, particularly his mother, disapprove strongly of Davy's choice of peer group. In addition, the family is shortly planning a move that will, by the physical distance imposed, sever Davy's peer relationships. Impulsively, Davy takes the family car and drives to a neighboring state without informing his parents. He returns with the car safely. Shortly after his return, Davy is taken to a mental health facility by his mother. The following interchange reveals the manner in which the Balascos react to the incident:

Mrs. Balasco: Well the first inclination that we had that Davy was having a problem was when he took the car right after school started and went on a joy ride for himself.

Mr. Balasco: I didn't know that he could drive . . . he drove all the way to another state.

Mrs. Balasco: He took the car . . . well thank God that he made it back and forth all right and it was very frightening to say the least that he would do something like that or even think of doing something that serious. And from there is when we found the different problems that he had within himself, so we decided to see if he could seek some help.

By taking a joy ride, Davy attempts to oppose his interactional role within the family as the sick child by demonstrating daring and precocious maturity. However, his behavior is impulsive and reflects poor judgment. Rather than helping him to attain increased relational distance from his parents; Davy's actions only serve to intensify his involvement in the family dialogue. Mrs. Balasco amplifies her caretaking posture and interacts with Davy as if he were a "sick" troubled child in need of immediate attention. Mr. Balasco remains detached and uninvolved with his "irresponsible" son. Thus, paradoxically, as Davy attempts to separate from his family, relational distance between Davy and his parents decreases. As relational distance decreases, Davy and his parents run the risk of the amplification of behavioral postures associated with separation and closeness, respectively. The family dialogue confronts the threat of stagnation as relating partners intensify their fixed complementary postures. In short, as Davy and his parents approach the task of adolescent separation, the Balasco family faces a serious crisis.

Comparative Summary: Past and Current Families

In summary, it is noteworthy to compare the Balascos' separation from their respective parents with Davy's current attempt to initiate a separation from his family. In their families of origin, separation between the Balascos and their parents occurs when complementary family interaction has reached a stalemate. Rather than being forced into a static role within the system, each of the Balascos chooses to leave the family. Their actions insure the perpetuation rather than the stagnation of their respective family dialogues. The leavetaking of each of the Balascos is facilitated by a strong identification with the "dominant" parent in each family. The "dominant" parent is the family member who most often strives to assume the behavioral posture associated with closeness. Their identification with the behavioral posture of this parent helps the Balascos to sustain flexible complementary interaction within the family system. That is, both Mr. and Mrs. Balasco are able to meet behavioral expectations associated with closeness and separation without risking amplification of the latter. In addition, their identification with the "dominant" parent provides the Balascos with a repertoire of behaviors which ultimately prove useful in helping them separate from their respective families. Mr. Balasco is able to separate from his family and immediately obtain employment at an "institution." Mrs. Balasco leaves home and chooses to live with a friend who needs help with an infant.

In the current Balasco family, separation is also provoked by an interactional stalemate. Mr. and Mrs. Balasco continue to interact with their youngest son, Davy, as if he were a sick child, when, in fact, he is growing to adulthood. Rather than be forced into this fixed relational position in the system, Davy chooses to leave the family. However, his lack of identification with either parent undermines the success of his efforts to separate. His joy ride proves to be an inadequate and irresponsible distancing mechanism. Davy returns home to find himself participating in a dialogue in which the behavioral postures associated with both closeness and separation are amplified further. Consequently, the potential for an interactional stalemate among this three-person systemic component increases. In short, the Balascos' initial involvement with Davy in relationships built on relatively fixed behavioral complementarity rather than on flexible or reciprical behavioral complementarity (the latter allowing for identification) ultimately threatens to terminate permanently their dialogue and to disrupt significantly the dynamic balance of the Balasco family system.

Adolescent Findings

The material collected in interviews with the adolescent participants is of a less comprehensive nature than that provided by the members of the Balasco family. Consequently, the task of identifying salient patterns of relational distance within the families of the adolescent participants was more difficult. The absence of parental narratives not only precluded a specific analysis of the transmission of relational patterns across generational boundaries, but also eliminated the opportunity to cross-validate relational structures through a comparison of perceptions made by the parents, the adolescent family members, and by the author. However, while the task of identifying relationships in the families of the adolescent participants was difficult, it was by no means impossible. The discussion earlier which focused on relational patterns in the Balascos' families of origin suggests that it is possible to reconstruct relational configurations in a family based upon the narrative of a single individual. A similar approach to the data was utilized here. The discussion reconstructed both the dialogue and the configuration of relationships associated with the task of distance minimization in the families of the adolescent participants prior to their suicide attempts. In order to simplify the current discussion, the dialogue for each of the two families under consideration will be identified prior to the presentation of the data itself. Excerpts from the narratives of two adolescent participants will then be examined against this background. Material from the narratives will be presented in chronological order, beginning with the adolescents' description of relationships and events in childhood and continuing to their perceptions of themselves and their relationships with others (most often family members) during adolescence and prior to their suicide attempts. In addition, the adolescents' descriptions of their parents will be included.

Nancy Franklin and Linda Petite, the two adolescents presented here are representative of the variability in the original adolescent sample; each falls at the opposite end of a behavioral continuum. Nancy Franklin presents as a tough youngster whose behavior during adolescence could be described as excessively rebellious. She dropped out of high school, ran away from home on numerous occasions, abused alcohol and drugs, and engaged in irresponsible sexual behavior (she had two abortions). In contrast, Linda Petite is a subdued, articulate youngster whose behavior in adolescence can best be described as conservative. She attended and completed high school, had no involvement with alcohol or drugs, did not engage in irresponsible sexual behavior, and did not participate in any outwardly rebellious activities. From these descriptions, the two girls appear to be quite different. However, an examination of their narratives reveals two striking similarities. Each girl plays an identical role in the family dialogue, and each girl occupies a similar position in the configuration of family relationships. Both Nancy Franklin and Linda Petite are intensely involved in minimizing familial distance.

Nancy Franklin

A review of Nancy's narrative highlights the complementary themes and corresponding behaviors which comprise the dialogue in the Franklin family. The specific motifs and behaviors associated with separation include helplessness, passivity, and emotional and physical vulnerability. The themes and behaviors linked with closeness include physical and emotional aggression. The dialogue is essentially sado-masochistic in nature; the infliction and reception of physical and emotional pain constituting complementarity of family interaction. It is against this thematic and interactional backdrop that Nancy's narrative will be examined, beginning with several of Nancy's more vivid childhood recollections.

Nancy's memories are of an unhappy and rocky childhood in which family members were always "picking fights with each other" but in particular "picking fights with me." She recalls, "I never fought back, because if I did they would go back and tell my father." Thus, early on, Nancy remembers assuming a helpless, passive, and physically vulnerable stance in her family. Notably she describes herself as different from her siblings in this respect; it is she, not they, who meets behavioral expectations associated with separation in the family.

Nancy's recollection of a childhood incident in which her mother flushed Nancy's pet gerbils down the toilet while Nancy was away at school further illustrates Nancy's position in the family. She recalls:

> It would be like somebody picked me up and dumped me into a river . . . like if I was young and couldn't defend myself and I knew that somebody was going to hurt me. The other kids wanted to keep them, but they didn't get as upset as me . . . my sister said that the gerbils wouldn't know the difference anyway . . . I was mad, . . . I went upstairs and started throwing things around and I didn't talk to anybody for a month.

Not only is Nancy the passive victim of separation from her pet gerbils, but she also appears to strongly identify with them and vicariously experiences herself as the helpless victim of a violent and cruel act. Again, it is Nancy and not her siblings who assumes a vulnerable position in the family. Although her siblings wanted to keep the gerbils, Nancy is the child whom the loss most pains.

School was yet another source of "pain" for Nancy. Because of an undetected hearing problem, school personnel assessed Nancy as intellectually limited and placed her in a special class "where most of the kids were mentally retarded." She recalls that in addition to being the object of cruelty from the kids at school, "my brothers made fun of me and even my mother would call me 'retarded.'" Here, both inside and outside the family, Nancy is the recipient of verbal cruelty and aggression from others. Within the family, Nancy assumes a complementary interactional position in relation to her mother and brothers; as they inflict emotional pain, she absorbs it.

Memories of Nancy's father dominate her description of her adolescence. She refers to him in the following manner:

> . . . him, I don't get along with at all. He can't sit down and have a simple conversation with you, he always yells . . . he gets mad, and hits me a lot . . . a couple of times he punched me in the head and the stomach, and he's given me black eyes and big lips.

In this and other excerpts from her narrative, Nancy depicts her father as exclusively assuming a behavioral posture associated with closeness in the family dialogue. She portrays him as verbally and physically aggressive, the primary inflictor of emotional and physical pain in the family. In turn, Nancy stresses that she is the major recipient of this pain. From her description, the two family members most involved in the family dialogue appear to be Nancy and her father.

References to her mother are rare in Nancy's narrative, particularly as she recollects adolescence. When asked to describe her mother, Nancy replies, "My mother, she's a bitch when she's drunk, you can't even say 'boo' to her." Generally, Nancy portrays her mother as an alcoholic who is hostile but distant and seemingly uninvolved with her. Thus, although the two women complement one another's behaviors, the quality of their interaction differs from Nancy's interaction with her father. While Mr. Franklin is frequently depicted as actively and directly aggressive in relation to his daughter, Mrs. Franklin is described as hostile and passive. Nancy cites many recollections in which her father inflicts physical pain on Nancy while Mrs. Franklin observes without comment or interest.

As Nancy approaches adolescence, her fantasies and dreams reflect her struggle with her behavioral role within the family. She states that at the age of 13, she considered murdering her mother but was afraid to go through with it because "my father would get me." Here Nancy attempts to avoid amplification of a posture in which she absorbs pain by considering inflicting pain. A similar motif occurs in a repetitive dream which begins when Nancy is 16. The dream involves:

> . . . people in my house, I didn't know who they were and we had this argument or fight or something and I just got really mad and I took a knife and started rubbing them out and then they take a knife and start stabbing me and I can see blood on them and blood on me and they would die but I wouldn't and I'd be walking around laughing.

In both the fantasy and the dream, Nancy strives to move out of her vulnerable, passive interactional posture by substituting other behaviors. However, these substitute behaviors are extreme, destructive, impulsive, and unrealistic. In fact, as Nancy faces the task of adolescent separation, she is ill-equipped to challenge the family's behavioral expectations. Her limited repertoire of behaviors undermines the extent to which she can negotiate a successful separation from her parents. The fixed complementary relationships in which Nancy and her parents have engaged since Nancy's childhood now face the danger of stagnation. Nancy's inadequate attempts to gain relational distance from her parents (e.g., running away from home) ultimately result in an amplification of complementary family interaction. Nancy's recollection of events when she ran away from home at the age of 17 illustrates this process. She recalls:

> I ran away because my father was always smacking me around for no reason at all and I wasn't getting along with the people in the house and I decided that if I left they'd be happier . . . so I left and my father got me the next day and he brought me home and it was my mother's day off so I knew she should be home and she wasn't and he locked the dog in the bedroom and he went into the living room and called me in and started beating me up.

She adds:

> . . . he's threatened me if I ever run away again, he's going to chain me in the cellar and beat me up every night . . . he's the kind of person that would do it. I don't think he'd do it to anybody else but me. My brother smokes pot and he just talks to him.

Nancy's comments not only illustrate the family's amplification of complementary behaviors as separation is attempted, but in addition point to Nancy's special role in the family dialogue (in contrast to her siblings) and to her position in the configuration of family relationships. Specifically, Nancy is the member of her family who most frequently assumes the behavioral posture associated with separation. She engages as such in fixed complementary relationships with both parents, although she seems to be more intensely involved in this way with her father. Thus, as Nancy and her parents approach the developmental task of adolescence, they are ill-prepared to negotiate a separation. Instead, as the system is forced to deal with separation, relational distance is discouraged and the family dialogue is threatened by stagnation. In short, the Franklin family system faces a serious relational crisis.

Linda Petite

Careful consideration of Linda's narrative illuminates the complementary themes and corresponding behaviors which constitute the dialogue in the Petite family. The primary themes and behaviors linked to separation are isolation, exclusion, helplessness, inadequacy, and emotional vulnerability. The major motifs and behaviors associated with closeness include involvement, inclusion, competency, responsibility, and emotional strength. These themes and behaviors will provide the backdrop against which Linda's narrative will be addressed. The discussion will begin by examining recollections of her early childhood years.

Linda's earliest memories involve feelings of exclusion, inadequacy, and helplessness at school. She recalls:

> I can remember back in kindergarten . . . doing my paper wrong . . . and the teacher looked at me funny and I can remember some of the kids laughing at me and I remember that they were all making newspaper bears and I couldn't and I don't know why . . . Another time I thought that I was late for class because they had morning sessions and afternoon sessions and I was crying because I didn't see anybody outside the school yard or anything and I saw kids in class and I couldn't get in, so I was crying and I went home and my mother said, "You're not late, you're early."

In the first of these two recollections, Linda describes other children as involved in a group activity. In contrast, she experiences herself as excluded and isolated. Notably, the basis of her exclusion is her incompetency. Thus, as opposed to the other children who form a competent involved group, Linda depicts herself as an incompetent, emotionally vulnerable isolate. In the second recollection, Linda describes another situation in which she is isolated and inadequate. Here, her mother's knowing competent stance complements Linda's uninformed, inadequate emotionally vulnerable position. In both recollections, Linda portrays herself as consistently meeting behavioral expectations associated with separation in the family dialogue.

Linda's memories of later school years are thematically congruent with her earlier recollections. She remembers:

> When I was younger, I got beaten up a lot and I wouldn't fight back because it wasn't my thing and I would cry and that is how I got my anger out and I was very frustrated. A lot of times at school it was let's pick on Linda today . . . everybody made it hard for me, teachers and students.

Here again, Linda depicts herself as a helpless, emotionally vulnerable, isolated child who is excluded from a group "involved" in "picking on" her.

As Linda describes herself in relation to members of her family, similar themes reappear. She explains:

> I kind of feel like I'm different from all of them because they always got involved in things which I never did . . . and I have different beliefs from my brothers because they're guys and from my sister Kathy because she's younger.

While her siblings are "involved in things," thereby meeting behavioral expectations associated with closeness in the family, Linda is excluded, isolated, and different.

In her narrative, Linda portrays herself as complementing the behavioral posture of her parents as well as the posture of her siblings. For example, she recalls:

> When I was growing up, I just wanted to be accepted by my parents, just like everybody else in the family.

In this and other excerpts, Linda conveys a sense of isolation in relation to her parents. In addition, she often describes them, particularly her mother, as involved with the family, while Linda remains an outsider. Linda appears to view her mother as the "dominant" parent or the family member most involved in meeting behavioral expectations associated with closeness. Mrs. Petite is the parent most frequently and descriptively referred to in Linda's narrative. Allusions to Mr. Petite are less frequent and notably vague. The following excerpts are illustrative:

> My mother . . . she's very sensitive, I feel that she takes a lot . . . she does a lot too . . . too much . . . she takes care of the house and the kids . . .

> My father . . . he's kind and he's a good father . . . I'm not sure why.

> Sometimes I feel like my mother does too much . . . I mean things that my father should be doing . . . it's like she's playing two roles . . . like when we go on vacation, I think that my father should be the one to make the reservations and things like that, but he hands the check over to my mother and she does it . . . My mother has always disciplined us, but it's funny, my father's the law . . . he's kind of stubborn old school. He'll just be angry . . . like sometimes when he's feeling sad, he'll just show anger.

Thus, as Linda describes herself throughout her narrative as the excluded, isolated, helpless, and inadequate child, she depicts her parents, and more specifically her mother, as involved, competent, and responsible. To the extent that they meet contrasting behavioral expectations, Linda and her mother appear to be the two family members most involved in the family dialogue.

As Linda encounters adolescence and is faced with the task of separation, her struggle with her behavioral role in the family is evidenced. The following statement is illustrative:

> Sometimes I feel like I belong in my family and sometimes I don't . . . sometimes I don't feel like I belong anywhere . . . sometimes I feel like I'm the only person in the world and that these are just people that I've created in my mind. That I'm not really living, it's only a dream.

Here, Linda vacillates between feeling included and excluded. Notably, in her inner world, she amplifies the latter feeling to the point of "not . . . living" or death. Although she struggles to avoid amplification of this, and other feelings and behaviors, her repertoire of replacement behaviors has been severely limited by the fixed complementary relationships in which she has previously engaged with her parents. Because she has consistently been delegated to assume the behavioral posture associated with separation in the family dialogue, she has had little opportunity to learn alternative behaviors and feelings. Her limited behavior choices undermine the extent to which she can negotiate a successful separation from her parents. Although Linda contends, "I can't take it when somebody tries to put me in a special place where they think that they are better than me," she is ill-equipped behaviorally to struggle out of such a "special place."

Unlike Davy Balasco and Nancy Franklin, both of whom attempt to attain relational distance from their respective parents through external action, Linda Petite's fight for separation is largely an internal one. As Linda attempts to feel differently about herself and behave accordingly within the family, the family dialogue intensifies. The following excerpt exemplifies this process:

> . . . like when I wanted to make my own decisions . . . they gave me a hassle . . . even if it didn't involve them, they didn't want to let me think for myself . . . they would always put me down . . . I would argue a lot with my mother. They never gave my brothers any hassle . . . my mother always let them go where they wanted . . . especially when they got older.

These statements not only highlight the family's amplification of complementary behavioral postures as Linda grows older and separation is attempted, but they also illuminate Linda's special part in the family dialogue (in contrast to her siblings) and her special position in the configuration of family relationships. Specifically, Linda appears to be the member of her family who most often meets behavioral expectations associated with separation. She engages as such in fixed complementary relationships with both parents, although she seems more intensely involved in this way with her mother. Thus, as Linda and her parents approach the task of separation, they are ill-prepared to negotiate relational distance. Rather, the complementary sets of behaviors which function to maintain familial relationships are intensified, and the stagnation threatens the family dialogue.

Summary of Family and Adolescent Findings

In overview, the relationship patterns described by the Balascos in their respective families of origin and in their current family, and those described by the two adolescent participants are remarkably similar. All of the families appear to be highly invested in minimizing intrafamilial distance. Members of each family system address the task within the context of a dialogue composed of themes and behaviors specific to their family. Generally, the data suggest that although separation and loss remain sensitive issues for all of these systems, family members are able to initiate and tolerate some familial separations while painfully and passively submitting to others. The amont of difficulty experienced by family members around any given separation appears related to the importance of the separating individual's role in the family dialogue and position in the configuration of family relationships. The greater the importance of the separating family member in these areas, the greater the chance for disruption of the family dialogue and significant alteration of the system's dynamic balance.

Mr. and Mrs. Balasco and the adolescent participants (including Davy Balasco) appear to play an important role in the family dialogue and appear to occupy a special position in the configuration of family relationships. Each of these individuals and his or her respective parents constitute a three-person system which ultimately is most responsible for minimizing intrafamilial distance (i.e., sustaining complementary interaction within the family context). The data reveal that the participants perceive the relationships which compose this three-person system as based either on identification or complementarity. Although Mr. and Mrs. Balasco engaged in reciprocal complementary relationships with their respective parents, the Balascos are unable to experience themselves as involved in this way. Rather, each of the Balascos perceives contrasting dyadic relational structures in which he or she strongly identifies with the behaviors of one parent while complementing the behaviors of the other. Notably, both Mr. and Mrs. Balasco strongly identify with the "dominant" parent in their families, or the parent whom they perceive as most frequently assuming the behavioral posture associated with closeness in the family dialogue. While the Balascos describe roles in the family dialogue that permitted some degree of behavioral flexibility, the adolescent participants convey a more constricted sense of family interaction. The adolescent participants describe familial relationships, particularly those between themselves and their respective parents as based on relatively fixed complementarity. The adolescents portray their parents as always assuming the behavioral postures associated with closeness, while they depict themselves as consistently assuming the behavioral posture linked to separation. Like the Balascos, the adolescent participants seem to have difficulty experiencing themselves as involved in a three person process. As they describe the relationships which compose the three person system, the adolescent participants all indicate that they feel significantly more involved with one parent than with the other in the family dialogue. Notably, the adolescents are more involved in this way with the "dominant" parent in their families. However, in contrast to the Balascos, none of the dyadic relational structures described by the adolescent participants are based on identification.

As all of the systems under examination here face the age appropriate separation of family members, numerous family interactional processes are highlighted. It seems clear that these systems experience the most difficulty when confronted with the separation of the child most involved in the family dialogue. As these very important children attempt to separate from their families, complementary family interaction intensifies as the three-person system strives to minimize intrafamilial distance and avoid separation and loss. Paradoxically, this amplification of contrasting behavioral postures poses a threat to the family system in the form of stagnation. A dialogue cannot be sustained if a posture or a set of behavioral expectations is amplified to a point at which the potential for complementarity with another posture or set of expectations is precluded. Notably, Mr. and Mrs. Balasco are able to protect their original families from interactional stagnation by decreasing their own involvement in the family dialogue. Although the Balascos only attain a limited degree of relational distance as they separate from their parents, the distancing process allows the family dialogue to continue albeit on a qualitatively and structurally different level. The Balascos are able to negotiate this type of separation because of the nature of their parental relationships. The Balascos' strong identification with their "dominant" parent supplements their interactional repertoire with behaviors associated with closeness in the family dialogue.

In contrast, the adolescent participants and their families experience more difficulty as they approach age appropriate separation. Stagnation of the family dialogue is a significantly greater threat, as these participants have fewer alternatives than the Balascos with which to avoid amplification of behavioral expectations. This unavailability of alternative behaviors stems from the nature of the relationships between these adolescents and their parents. As interactional roles within their families were relatively fixed, these adolescents had fewer opportunities to oppose the behaviors associated with separation by identifying with behaviors associated with closeness. As a result, these adolescents and their parents are ill-equipped to negotiate a separation and still sustain (although in an altered form) the family dialogue. These systems face major changes in the dynamic balance of familial relationships; crisis appears imminent.

6

Mastering Loss:
The Meaning Of Relationships

In this chapter, the focus shifts from the identification of familial patterns to a deeper understanding of the relationships in families with a suicidal adolescent member. A closer look at the relationship patterns isolated in chapter 5 suggests that a similar relational process plays an integral part in the lives of the families under consideration. Specifically, issues of identity and power are foreground in the determination of the qualitative and structural characteristics of this process.

Within their respective theoretical frameworks, both Nagy (1973) and Kantor (1975) discuss and assess numerous relational patterns including patterns similar to those found in the families of the participants. Each theorist points to the limitations which such patterns place on the process of relating. The comments of Nagy are particularly relevant when considering the fixed role complementarity which characterizes the familial relationships of the participants. Nagy notes that although relational roles may appear to be opposites, a relationship is not composed of a genuinely antithetical dialogue unless reciprocity between the roles or the behaviors of the relating partners exists. Relationships which lack such reciprocity are typified by a "polarized fusion of roles." Bipolar fusion in a relationship eliminates the potential for "creative synthesis" or the genuine sharing of contributions by relating partners. Nagy contends, rather, that family members in polarized roles become "vicariously dependent on one another's function in such a manner that neither faces his own relational world as a whole person." Thus, relating partners are "fused" and cannot experience each other in a genuinely intimate or separate manner.

Kantor's remarks are applicable in addressing the way in which the participants' relationships restrict their ability to attain qualitative or relational distance. Generally, Kantor stresses the importance of a balanced interplay between the family's and the individual's conceptual, affective, and volitional experiences. Healthy family relationships must be flexible, adaptable, and negotiable. The more that family members are willing to encourage, permit, and accept individual differences while still providing shared qualitative family experience, the greater the ease with which family members can adapt to life inside and outside the family sphere. In contrast, Kantor contends that systems in which a primary emphasis is placed on family beliefs, family emotional needs, and family efficacy at the expense of the individual are those in which the quality of both intimacy and separateness is diminished. Families, such as those of the participants, appear to give priority to family functioning and to discourage the attainment of individual differences. These systems seem to be typified by a relational process which is shaped more by family need rather than an interplay between family and individual needs. In short, both Nagy and Kantor note that relational patterns similar to those found in the participants' families may interfere substantially with the ability of individuals to experience genuine intimacy and separateness within the context of family relationships. In addition, the theorists' comments suggest that relationships in these families are determined more by dependency or need than by choice.

Bowen (1976) describes individuals whose functioning is determined more by need than by choice as having a lower degree of integration of "self." Such individuals experience a fusion or lack of differentiation between their emotional system—instinctual needs and experiences such as hunger, contentment, fear, and agitation—and their intellectual system—cognitive functions and experiences such as reasoning, thinking, and reflecting. Bowen contends that the greater the fusion between these two systems, the less the individual is able to make decisions and choices based on logic and careful thought, and the more likely the individual is to have his or her actions dictated by emotional states. Consequently, such individuals are less flexible, less adaptable, and disproportionately dependent on others to meet their emotional needs. Bowen suggests that individuals become more "relationship-oriented" as their degree of differentiation decreases; thus, these individuals become over-dependent on relationships for emotional confirmation. As the amount of emotional investment in relationships increases, the extent to which individuals seek confirmation of other aspects of their experience within relationships also increases. For example, within the family context, poorly differentiated family members who are over-reliant on familial relationships for emotional confirmation will be more likely to remain bound to family relationships within the experiential realms of "Meaning" and "Power." That is, rather than feeling free to explore different options regarding conceptual and volitional experiences, these individuals would feel tied to the family by emotional needs and, consequently, would be more likely to adopt family values, ideologies, and hierarchical volitional positions. As differentiation decreases, individuals are increasingly bound to the family for confirmation of identity in all areas of experience and are less able to establish identities outside the context of family relationships. Generally, the poorer the integration of self, the more that identity requires definition within the context of a relationship; thus, the more tenuous and ill-defined that identity itself becomes outside of relational boundaries.

As the participants in the inquiry speak about separation and loss, or the termination of relationships, they associate to an experience that is so disruptive that their survival is threatened. Reexamination of the data suggests that, in fact, separation and loss represent not only the actual structural termination of relationships but also potential loss of identity itself. From this perspective, the need to minimize distance or to maintain relationships may be understood as a way of insuring the confirmation of identity.

Further examination of the relational patterns which typify the families of the participants highlights the manner in which power is used to insure the continuation of relationships. Kantor notes that it is within the field of "Power" that family members "get things done" or accomplish mutual goals. He argues that "learning, exercising, and striving for mastery of skills are all a part of a family's efforts to be effective." Within a family system, positions of power are hierarchical— some family members are delegated more responsibility than others and, consequently, use their power to accomplish family goals. Optimally, the experience of power will be a flexible and negotiable one in which all family members are given the opportunity to increase their learning and mastery of skills. As illustrated in the present study, the quality of the participants' relationships is notably rigid and inflexible within all of the experiential dimensions including the dimension of "Power." In the families of the participants, power is delegated and maintained in such an inflexible manner that the hierarchical positions held by family members remain relatively fixed. Within the trio of family members most responsible for minimizing distance, greater power resides with the parents than with the involved offspring. The extreme way in which these parents maintain a relatively powerful position in relation to the less powerful position of the child undermines the potential for increased relational distance, or separation, and thus insures the continuity of the trio of relationships. As family members adhere to hierarchical position, their identities are confirmed by the conceptual and affective qualities associated with these position.

In summary, it is apparent that what has been referred to previously in the discussion as the process of "minimizing distance" has a more specific meaning. This meaning is evidenced in the interplay between identity confirmation and the use of power. The relating process in which the participants and their families engage would be more properly termed "mastering loss." Ordinarily, "mastering loss" connotes a positive process through which individuals work through, or master the painful effects associated with actual events of loss. However, for the participants in this inquiry, "mastering loss" appears in a more dysfunctional light. Within the context of this investigation, "loss" has been equated not just with the loss of others, but with the loss of identity. "Mastering" refers to the rigid use of power in conjunction with goal attainment. "Mastering loss" is a process through which an individual confirms identity through the occupation of a position of power in relation to another individual who occupies a less powerful position and who consequently is less able to confirm identity. The two positions involved in the process represent the complementary behavioral postures identified earlier in the family dialogues of the participants. Behavioral expectations associated with separation are synonomous with the "loss" position, while behavioral expectations associated with closeness represent the "mastering" position.

The efficacy of the process of "mastering loss" is dependent on the ability of relating individuals to sustain behavioral complementarity and to avoid role stagnation or relationship termination. The latter would occur if behaviors associated with either the "loss" or the "mastering" positions were intensified or amplified to such a point that the potential for complementarity with the opposite set of behaviors would be eliminated. In families engaged in "mastering loss," systemic dynamic balance is reflected in the quality of the interplay between the behavioral postures associated with "loss" and "mastering," respectively. The more that relating individuals are able to interchangeably meet behavioral expectations associated with both positions, the greater the flexibility of the family relational structure, and consequently the more stable the relationship system. As the range of contrasting behavioral postures available to relating partners becomes limited, the relational structure of the family becomes more rigid, and the stability of the system more tenuous.

Notably, as relating partners become less differentiated, they exhibit a greater need for identity confirmation within relationships and, thus, intensify their involvement in the "mastering" process. Intensification of "mastering" behaviors demands an equal intensification of "loss" behaviors in order to insure behavioral complementarity. Such intensification leads to a more rigid relational structure which, in turn, increases the risk of role stagnation or relationship termination (i.e., loss of identity). Thus, the process of "mastering loss" appears to have the potential to function in a paradoxically undermining manner.

Mastering Loss in the Family System: An Historical-Developmental Model

The process of "mastering loss" appears to make an important contribution to systemic functioning in the families of the participants. In order to better understand the nature of this contribution, the discussion will first consider "mastering loss" within a broad developmental framework and, second, view this process in relation to salient theoretical constructs from the historical-developmental model of Murray Bowen.

The Role of Development

By nature, the family offers configurations of relationships that are particularly adaptable to the process of "mastering loss." Parent-child relationships represen the coupling of the qualitative and structural patterns inherent in the relational process under consideration. On a developmental continuum, the child and the parent denote contrasting degrees of differentiation of self. Children are dominated primarily by what Bowen refers to as the "automatic emotional system." That is, the behaviors of children are motivated more by instinctual and emotional needs and mediated less by intellectual processes such as thinking and reasoning. Children are, by necessity, relationship-oriented; they are less capable of attaining goals on their own and of developing a sense of efficacy in relation to their environment. In short, children occupy a developmental position in which identity is in the primary stages of formation, and power over the external world is limited. In contrast, parents by virtue of biologic growth and greater cognitive maturity have developed into individuals who can assert more control over the environment, and thereby can more effectively attain goals. In comparison to the child, the parent represents a higher level of identity formation and possesses a greater degree of power. The developmental distinctions between the parent-child roles gradually diminish as the child grows and begins to develop higher order cognitive skills which, in turn, facilitate an experience of mastery of the environment.

Adolescence is the developmental period in which family members and society at large formally begin to de-emphasize the distinction between parent-child relational roles. Adolescence represents the bridge between childhood and adulthood. It is the time when the child begins to solidify an identity outside the context of familial relationships and the time when mastery over the environment increases significantly. The role changes associated with adolescence are stressful for any family; however, the greater the degree of relational flexibility and adaptability within the family system, the better the chance for a successful negotiation of this developmental task.

Families in which the parents are moving towards decreasing degrees of differentiation initially tend to make rigid the already inherent qualitative and structural patterns of the parent-child relationship. The need of these parents for constant confirmation of identity in conjunction with a relational role results in a perpetuation of parent-child role distinctions. Interchangeability of behaviors within the relationship are poorly tolerated and the child's attempts to psychologically grow by developing identity and by gaining mastery over the environment are discouraged. The child predominantly enacts behaviors associated with separation, while the parents meet behavioral expectations associated with closeness. Thus, the child occupies the "loss" position and the parents, the "mastering" position.

In these families, the adolescent period of development proves difficult. The extent to which family members rely on the occupation of relatively fixed roles for the confirmation of identity makes the prospect of role change a threatening one. Parents who experience adolescent separation as threatening intensify their occupation of the "mastering" position, thereby demanding a corresponding amount of intensification from the adolescent in the "loss" position. Ultimately, the nature of the relationship between the adolescent and his or her parents earlier in life determines the quality of the separation in adolescence. The greater the degree of earlier relational rigidity, the higher the chances that the "mastering loss" process will be intensified during adolescence. As this process is intensified, the parent-adolescent separation is undermined. Although these adolescents and their parents may separate in space, the qualitative nature of their separateness is limited. Poorly differentiated adolescents are more apt to separate from their families only to recapitulate dysfunctional family patterns in relationships outside the family context. This recapitulation of family patterns belies the superficiality of the separation and underscores the extent to which the adolescent is still tied to familial relationships.

A Bowenian perspective

Bowen (1976) provides an historical-developmental model which is generally applicable to understanding the process of "mastering loss" as it contributes to systemic functioning in the families of the participants. Bowen's concepts are helpful in assessing the range and efficacy of family functioning both within the current and past generations. In addition, Bowen offers a theoretical context within which to predict the perpetuation of salient patterns of family function across generational boundaries. Bowen's framework consists of a number of theoretical constructs which contribute in an interdependent manner to the dynamic and structural manifestations of family systems. For the purpose of discussion, these constructs have been divided into three categories: anxiety, concepts relating to level of individual differentiation, and concepts pertaining more specifically to systemic processes and structure. The discussion will present a brief synopsis of these three categories. Following each of these synopses, the relevance of Bowen's concepts to the process of "mastering loss" will be examined.

Anxiety. Anxiety is a major cornerstone of Bowen's theoretical framework; he views it as a catalyst of individual and systemic dysfunction. Bowen argues that anxiety is an emotional state that signals a threat to survival for the lower organisms as well as for higher forms of life. While he notes that most organisms are equipped to handle acute periods of anxiety without manifesting lasting signs of distress or dysfunction, he contends that the presence of chronic anxiety can prove problematic for any individual. Bowen asserts that individuals with lower levels of differentiation are more vulnerable to long periods of intense anxiety. The interaction between low level of integration of self and sustained anxiety can result in dysfunction within the individual as well as within the individual's relationship system. Dysfunction refers to an increase in the level of fusion between the intellectual and emotional systems. Individual dysfunction results in a decrease in the level of differentiation and systemic dysfunction results in a decrease in the level of differentiation for one or more individuals. Often, the degree of individual dysfunction is covert and cannot be assessed until the individual is forced to function apart from the relationship system.

Because they move towards decreasing degrees of differentiation, individuals engaged in the process of "mastering loss" are more vulnerable to chronic anxiety. These individuals will experience anxiety as a significant and enduring threat to identity. Anxiety marks a return to the more instinctually determined "automatic emotional" state which these individuals associate with a loss of defined self. As anxiety heightens the threat of loss for these individuals, it will simultaneously trigger the need for more intense involvement in the process of "mastering loss." Consequently, chronically anxious individuals with low levels of differentiation will tend to rigidify relational roles and increase the risk of role stagnation. In turn, the likelihood of relationship termination and additional dysfunction will increase. Thus, anxiety represents a variable that can intensify the process of "mastering loss" and, in the manner described above, undermine its effectiveness.

Assessing individual levels of differentiation: The emotional cut-off. Bowen contends that one of the most effective ways to assess an individual's level of differentiation is to examine the manner in which the individual functions apart from his or her family of origin. More specifically, he believes that careful scrutiny of the way in which an individual separates from his or her past to begin life in the present reveals the level of unresolved emotional attachment to one's parents. The degree of unresolved emotional attachment is synonymous with an individual's level of differentiation.

Bowen terms the manner in which individuals separate from the past the "emotional cut-off" and determines the severity of the "cut-off" by studying the quality and intensity of separation from the family of origin. He postulates that unresolved emotional attachment is handled either by "the intrapsychic process of denial and isolation of self while living close to the parents or by physically running away; or by both emotional isolation and physical distance." Individuals who remain nearby tend to have some degree of supportive contact with their parents. These individuals "cut-off" from their families by creating emotional distance and tend to respond to prolonged anxiety with internalized symptoms such as physical and emotional illness. Individuals who run away "cut-off" from their parents by creating geographical distance. These individuals tend to see the problem as residing in their parents and respond to chronic anxiety with impulsive behavior and externalized symptoms.

Bowen contends that the presence of anxiety results in an increase in the intensity of the "emotional cut-off." The severity of the "cut-off" serves as an indicator of the level of systemic differentiation in past generations and as a predictor of the amount of differentiation that they will carry over to future generations. Finally, Bowen argues that although there are many gradations of "emotional cut-off," the more an individual maintains some kind of "viable emotional contact" with the past generation, the less likely that a lower level of differentiation will appear in the next generation.

Within the present context, scrutiny of the emotional cut-off during and after the adolescent phase of development facilitates the identification of the families engaged in the process of "mastering loss." In addition, consideration of the cut-off aids in an assessment of the efficacy of the process of "mastering loss" in a given family. An examination of the nature of the cut-off reveals the extent to which parent-child relationships were rigidified earlier in family life. The more extensive the emotional or physical distance between an individual and his or her parents, the greater the likelihood of earlier role rigidification and, consequently, the more precarious the process of "mastering loss." Individual extremes in either emotional or physical isolation reflect a higher degree of unresolved parental attachment and a lower level of integration of self. In short, the more severe the cut-off, the more threatened the efficacy of the task of "mastering loss" and the more likely that the individuals involved will experience internalized and/or relational dysfunction in the future.

Systemic processes and structure: Marriage. Bowen notes that the formation of a family system in the present begins as individuals with similar degrees of differentiation seek each other out for marriage. The lower the level of individual differentiation, the greater the potential for systemic dysfunction in the future, and the more intense the emotional fusion in the marriage. The degree of emotional fusion results in varying levels of chronic anxiety for one or both spouses. Bowen argues that in an on-going marital relationship, one spouse usually assumes the role of the dominant decision-maker, while the other spouse adopts a more adaptive position. He stresses that these roles are not determined by gender but, rather, by the position that each of the spouses occupied in their respective families of origin. The anxiety which results from the degree of emotional fusion in the marriage may be managed in a number of ways including emotional distance between the spouses, marital conflict, sickness or dysfunction in one spouse, or a projection of problems onto children. Systemic dysfunction may be focused in one of these areas or distributed in varying degrees to all. The more that dysfunction is focused in one area, the less that the other areas will be impaired or vulnerable to dysfunction in the future. The distribution of systemic dysfunction is derived from the distribution patterns in the families of origin of the spouses and is determined by the level of differentiation in the current spouse system.

From the perspective of the current study, it is likely that individuals with similar degrees of involvement in the task of "mastering loss" in their families of origin will seek each other out for marriage. The marital relationship provides a potential context within which to confirm identity. The amount of emotional fusion and related anxiety in the marital relationship reflects the extent to which the spouses rely on rigid role structures to confirm identity. The absence of reified roles within the marital relationship may prove anxiety-arousing for the spouses as the confirmation of identity via the occupation of a position of power is not assured. Most likely, both of the spouses perceive themselves as occupying the position associated with identity confirmation (i.e., the "mastering" position) in some aspect of marital functioning. However, one spouse may have greater need for identity confirmation and, thus, may rigidly adhere to a more powerful position in several areas of marital or family functioning while the other spouse occupies a less powerful position more often. The anxiety which stems from the emotional fusion in the marriage may result in an intensification of the "mastering" process. This intensification could lead to further rigidification of marital roles and consequently increase the marital system's vulnerability to dysfunction. Thus, systemic dysfunction resulting from fusion anxiety would signal a decrease in the efficacy of the task of "mastering loss." Spouses may attempt to avoid role stagnation and the ultimate termination of the marital relationship in a number of ways including emotional distance, marital conflict in which the positions of "mastering" and "loss" are interchanged, spouse dysfunction in which marital roles become rigidified in an adult-child paradigm, and projection onto the children in which the roles occupied by the offspring become rigid in varying degrees depending on the level of parental differentiation.

Systemic processes and structure: Parent-child relationships. Bowen refers to the projection of dysfunction onto the children as the family projection process (FPP) and notes that the process "is so universal that it is present to some degree in all families." He argues that there are definite patterns in which dysfunction is distributed to the children. First, it may be distributed to one child and if the level of dysfunction is too great for that child, it will be distributed to other children in lesser degrees. The way in which the child becomes the target of the FPP is related to the level of differentiation of the parents, the amount of anxiety at the time of conception and birth, and the orientation of the parents towards marriage and children. In families in which the level of parental differentiation is lower, a selection of a child for the projection of dysfunction may be determined by additional factors such as birth order or special meaning attached to the child by the parents. The major factor involved in the FPP is the amount of emotional investment, or the "automatic emotional response" that the parent feels towards the child. An intense degree of emotional fusion may exist between the mother and child and not be manifested in overt dysfunction until the period of adolescence when the child attempts to function apart from the family. At that point, dysfunction may become visible in the child's relationship with either parent.

Within the context of the present inquiry, the FPP may be seen as an adaptation of a parent-child relationship to the process of "mastering loss." Here, one or more children occupy the "loss" position in the family as one or both parents assuage anxiety by claiming the "mastering" position. The degree of dysfunction in such relationships may not be discernible until the onset of adolescence when the distinctions between parent-child roles are normally deemphasized. Because the continuation of the process of "mastering loss" requires the maintenance of relationships, the child chosen for primary involvement in the process may not always be the child who emerges from the family with the lowest level of individual differentiation. There may be some children in the family who adhere too strictly to the "loss" position (e.g., children with physical disability) and, thus, are limited in the level of integration of the emotional and cognitive systems which they can achieve. The process of "mastering loss" requires the participation of a child who can occupy the "loss" position without amplifying the behaviors associated with it. This child must contribute to the perpetuation rather than the termination of the relationship. Thus, while certain children may rigidly occupy the "loss" position in the family thereby failing to increase their level of differentiation through development, they will not necessarily be the children in whom the parents have the most emotional investment. However, to the extent that the parents are able to diffuse dysfunction among different children, the less reliant they will be on reification of structure in one particular parent-child relationship. Consequently, the process of "mastering loss" will be a more effective one within the system. Nonetheless, the child who is the primary target of the FPP will emerge from the family with a level of differentiation lower than that of his or her parents and will be more relationship dependent and more vulnerable to dysfunction in the future.

To briefly summarize, Bowen recognizes the on-going nature of family process. He contends that aspects of family functioning transcend generational boundaries and he has developed theoretical constructs that prove useful both in delineating patterns of function and in capturing their motion and influence over long periods of time. Bowen argues that the use of his constructs in combination with detailed historical information and knowledge of the present family system can facilitate a reconstruction of the major processes at work within a family from one generation to the next. Thus, Bowen's approach is particularly adaptable to the study of the process of "mastering loss" both within and across generational boundaries. The historical information as well as the extensive nature of the material which the Balascos provided about their current family facilitates a reconstruction of the process of "mastering loss" as it contributes to general family functioning across generational boundaries. Although less extensive, the information provided by the adolescent participants permits a reconstruction of the process of "mastering loss" as it contributes to family functioning within the present generation. The following discussion reviews pertinent aspects of the narratives of the Balasco family and the adolescent participants in order to illuminate the role that the process of "mastering loss" plays in determining the quality of systemic functioning. This overview, in turn, highlights the way in which this process leads to systemic dysfunction and thus provides a framework within which to understand adolescent suicidal behavior.

Mastering Loss in the Balasco Family: An Example of Multi-Generational Transmission

The interview data provided by the Balasco family illustrates how numerous factors such as anxiety, level of individual differentiation, and specific family structures and processes can effect the quality of systemic functioning. In particular, it shows the way in which the interaction of these factors can directly determine the efficacy with which the process of "mastering loss" is carried out across generational boundaries. The effectiveness of the process is reflected in the quantity and quality of covert and overt systemic dysfunction. As the process of "mastering loss" becomes less effective, the likelihood of overt manifestations of systemic dysfunction increases. The discussion to follow will reconstruct the quality of functioning in the past and present family systems of the Balascos. As the material is reconstructed, a picture of cross-generational deterioration of the process of "mastering loss" emerges and signs of family dysfunction become more readily visible.

Mr. Balasco: Mastering Loss in the Family of Origin

As Mr. Balasco describes individuals, events, and day-to-day existence on the farm in his family of origin, a degree of rigidification of parent-child relational roles is evident. His repeated references to the children as the "working machine" and the "workhorses" and his depiction of his parents and, in particular, his father as the overseer, conveys a sense of role rigidity within the family. Ethnic values and traditions frequent Mr. Balasco's memories of relational transactions and appear to be primary binding forces in parent-child relationships. Specific familial expectations for the "oldest boy" and the general Portuguese philosophy—"they brought you into the world and they figured from then on you must carry"—underscore this quality of role reification. The manner in which family members approach the developmental task of adolescence further evidences the relatively fixed aspects of early parent-child relationships. The extremity which characterizes the actions of several of the children as they attempt to separate from the family reflects the family's difficulty with the negotiation of role change.

Generally, Mr. Balasco's narrative suggests that the process of "mastering loss" plays a part in overall family functioning. However, the fact that parent-child separations occur within a context of relatively moderate disruption implies that familial role rigidification is not of an extreme nature and that the identities of family members are not totally dependent on or determined within the framework of systemic relationships. A degree of reciprocal behavior complementarity is permitted in parent-child relationships. Consequently, the process of "mastering loss" appears to function to stabilize family relationships and the extent of overt family dysfunction is minimal.

An examination of specific familial relationships suggests the factors that contribute to systemic stability in Mr. Balasco's family of origin. Given the historical information available, a reasonable argument can be made for Mr. Balasco's strong involvement in the family process of "mastering loss." An examination of the circumstances surrounding his birth, the general composition of the family, and Mr. Balasco's relational stance towards his parents during childhood, adolescence, and adulthood implies that he is the child who is the primary target of the FPP. Mr. Balasco's birth follows a period of parental trauma during which the two children who preceded Mr. Balasco in the birth order died at one and two years of age from diptheria. Although Mr. Balasco's parents may have experienced other periods of anxiety during their family life, the emphasis which Mr. Balasco places on the deaths suggests that the time preceding his birth was, indeed, the most anxiety provoking for his parents. Speculatively, the interaction of this chronic anxiety with the level of parental differentiation creates a moderate degree of systemic dysfunction in which Mr. Balasco's parents experience a threat to identity confirmation as their parental relationship with two of their children is abruptly terminated. Thus, Mr. Balasco is born at a time when his parents need to intensify their occupation of the "mastering" position and, in turn, need a child to occupy the "loss" position with equal intensity. Mr. Balasco becomes this child. In infancy, Mr. Balasco contracts the disease that killed his brothers and, thus, parental anxiety is heightened and covert systemic dysfunction increases. As a child who is near death, or identity negation and powerlessness, Mr. Balasco is barely able to sustain his position in the "mastering" process. As he nears amplification of his behavioral role, Mr. Balasco's relationship with his parents is threatened by termination. Mr. Balasco's survival offers his parents a firmer hold on identity—the parent-child relationship is secured and the process of "mastering loss" functions effectively once more for the family.

Mr. Balasco depicts himself during childhood and adolescence as an individual who develops many of the characteristics—physical stamina, affective stance, and ethnic values—associated with his parents and, more specifically, his father. The fact that Mr. Balasco is able to identify with his father suggests that rigidification of their parent-child relationship is not extreme and that a substantial degree of movement towards the adult or parental role is tolerated. No doubt, the range of behavioral reciprocity within the relationship between father and son is determined primarily by the level of paternal differentiation; however, the familial role occupied by Mr. Balasco's younger brother, Peter, also may have deflected the amount of dysfunction which otherwise might have been focused on Mr. Balasco' relationship with his father. Peter, younger than Mr. Balasco by three years contracts polio in early childhood and is paralyzed for life. Speculatively, his permanent disability allows him to absorb a degree of systemic dysfunction. His physical limitations facilitate his compliance with parental discouragement of growth and, thus, in comparison to his physically healthy siblings, Peter remains less differentiated and more rigidly bound to the role of a child. However, although Peter occupies a "loss" position in the family, his physical disability limits the extent to which he can avoid amplification of the behaviors associated with the position. Thus, his parents are not primarily invested in Peter as a partner in the process of "mastering loss."

Mr. Balasco's transition from childhood to adulthood is markedly free of outward signs of dysfunction. His departure to the Navy at age 17 is not a source of conflict within the family. This smooth leavetaking underscores the quality of Mr. Balasco's relationship with his parents and, particularly his father; role reification is moderate and a degree of behavioral reciprocity is permissible. Mr. Balasco can join the Navy to become "a man" and his father can remain at home and retain his identity as a farmer. As he leaves, Mr. Balasco still occupies the "loss" position (e.g., his father comments, "They're going to make a man out of you"), and his parents continue to experience themselves in the "mastering" position. Concurrently, when he leaves his family behind, Mr. Balasco thinks of himself as already "a man" (e.g., he comments to his father, "You've already done that in spades") and, thus, is able to occupy the "mastering" position while placing his parents in the "loss" position. The apparent success with which Mr. Balasco and his parents are able to orchestrate this separation reflects the effectiveness of the process of "mastering loss" in the family.

However, closer scrutiny of the circumstances which surround his early adulthood years, as well as a careful examination of Mr. Balasco's general emotional stance, is indicative of the level of covert systemic dysfunction; the nature of Mr. Balasco's emotional cut-off from his parents is notable. In the years following his departure from the farm, Mr. Balasco continues to maintain a degree of supportive contact with his parents at the expense of his own progress in life outside the family context. During this period, as well as later in life, Mr. Balasco's stance of emotional isolation and his denial of personal needs is marked. Refusing a promotion in the Navy, Mr. Balasco returns home to a deteriorated farm where he works without pay for more than three years. As he strives to "get the farm back" to its earlier productive state, his concurrent attempts to build a life for himself apart from the family are not successful. He experiences overt relational dysfunction as his first marriage becomes increasingly unstable and finally terminates in a divorce.

A careful examination of events during this time period strongly suggests that the degree of dysfunction in Mr. Balasco's life reflects the degree of concurrent systemic dysfunction in his family of origin. Mr. Balasco's parents are facing the final years of their life. The various contexts within which they have sought identity confirmation are gradually eliminated. All but two of the children have left home and the farm has deteriorated. Their identities as parents and farmers become increasingly precarious. In addition, the health of Mr. Balasco's mother begins to worsen significantly. As the threat of loss of identity increases, the process of "mastering loss" increases. Mr. Balasco reenters the system in the role of "workhorse" and his father resumes the authoritarian role of overseer; the earlier parent-child relational roles are called into play. However, in this situation, the efficacy of the process of "mastering loss" appears limited. Systemic anxiety and vulnerability to identify loss continue to increase and are outwardly reflected as tension builds between Mr. Balasco and his father. Parent-child roles become more and more rigid and permission for behavioral reciprocity decreases. Finally, his father takes away the fields of crops from him, and Mr. Balasco leaves the farm.

This interaction suggests that a continuation of the parent-child relationship as it existed prior to this time is not possible. A change in the parent-child relationship must, and does, occur. The two relational choices which Mr. Balasco's father pose to him are the two choices which confront the system. If Mr. Balasco remains on the farm, he faces the threat of behavioral amplification as his father literally strips him of any power through excessive role rigidification. In turn, the family system faces the threat of relationship termination. Thus, the process of "mastering loss" would completely break down. If Mr. Balasco leaves the farm, the parent-child relationship is altered but sustained. Initially, Mr. Balasco assumes the "mastering" position as he makes a life for himself away from home and his father assumes the "loss" position as he feels "despondent" over his son's departure. When Mr. Balasco returns to the farm to work for free on his days off, the original parent-child roles are resumed although on a qualitatively different level. Now, Mr. Balasco occasionally occupies the "loss" position and his father occasionally occupies the "mastering" position. Mr. Balasco's parents are still able to confirm identity within the context of family relationships, although not as effectively as in the system's earlier years.

The level of differentiation which characterizes the system throughout most of its life allows it to negotiate this separation without extreme signs of overt dysfunction. Mr. Balasco appears capable of seeking identity confirmation outside of his family of origin and his parents seem able to maintain a sense of identity without him. However, because Mr. Balasco is the primary target of the FPP, he emerges from the system with a level of differentiation that is lower than that of his parents. Consequently, his need to occupy the "mastering" position in relationships is more intense. As Mr. Balasco pursues the task of identity confirmation, he will run a greater risk of rigidifying relational roles and experiencing overt dysfunction in the form of relationship termination.

Mrs. Balasco: Mastering Loss in the Family of Origin

Mrs. Balasco's recollections of her family of origin are filled with allusions to sickness, physical disability, and caretaking. While these aspects of family life serve to keep the family "close," their presence in the system contributes to an overall quality of vulnerability. Parent-child role rigidification is striking. Due to their physical disabilities, many of the children come dangerously close to amplifying behaviors associated with the "loss" position. In response, Mrs. Balasco's parents experience a subtle but chronic level of anxiety as confirmation of their identities in the parental role or "mastering" position is tenuous. Consequently, the family, particularly in its earlier years of existence, is threatened by a pervasive sense of relationship termination, or loss of identity. The interplay between the behaviors associated with the "mastering" and "loss" positions, respectively, is unstable and the survival of the family system remains a subtle but continual question. The extent of unconditional parent-child role rigidification is underscored by the fact that several of the children never have the opportunity to negotiate the developmental task of adolescence. Nevertheless, the fact that George, one of the older healthier children, is able to leave the family during his adolescent period suggests that, although the system was sensitive to loss, willful separations were not impossible. However, the extremity which characterizes George's actions as he separates from the family points to the family's difficulty accepting role changes.

In general, Mrs. Balasco's narrative suggests that due to circumstances, the process of "mastering loss" plays a pervasive role in the overall functioning of the family. Extreme role rigidification and relationship termination (e.g., the forced separation of Evelyn from the family) are not uncommon in Mrs. Balasco's family of origin. The identities of many family members are determined exclusively in relation to the family system and, consequently, the system manifests both covert and overt signs of dysfunction. An overview of specific events and familial relationships delineates the factors which contribute to functioning in Mrs. Balasco's family of origin.

Given the available historical information, a strong argument can be posed for Mrs. Balasco's extensive involvement in the family process of "mastering loss." An analysis of the circumstances surrounding her birth, the general composition of the family, and Mrs. Balasco's relational stance towards her parents and family during childhood, adolescence, and adulthood implies that she is the child who is the primary target of the FPP. Mrs. Balasco's birth is the product of extreme family trauma. She is born a premature and sickly baby shortly after the family's oldest child, Alan, is hit by a truck and killed. Alan's loss is experienced by Mrs. Balasco's parents as an abrupt and premature termination of a parent-child relationship, and more specifically as the result of their inadequacy in the parenting role. The chronic anxiety created by this trauma interacts with the existing level of parental differentiation and results in a substantial degree of covert systemic dysfunction as Mrs. Balasco's parents experience a serious threat to their identities. Mrs. Balasco is born during a period in the family's life when her parents desperately need to intensify their occupation of the "mastering" position and, in turn, require a child to occupy the "loss" position with corresponding intensity. Mrs. Balasco becomes this child. As a sickly baby, Mrs. Balasco is barely able to sustain her position in the mastering process. As she nears amplification of her behavioral role, parental anxiety and covert systemic dysfunction is heightened further. When Mrs. Balasco's precarious physical condition improves, Mrs. Balasco offers her parents a firmer hold on their identities. The process of "mastering loss" functions more effectively as the parent-child relationship becomes more secure. However, the subtle level of chronic anxiety which pervades family functioning earlier remains. No doubt it substantially increases when Mrs. Balasco's older brother, Jimmy, contracts rheumatic fever at the age of six and thereafter suffers for years from serious physical debilitation. His almost unconditional occupation of the "loss" position serves to undercut the efficacy of the process of "mastering loss" in the family and covert systemic dysfunction increases.

Mrs. Balasco depicts herself as a child who develops the primary characteristics associated with her mother. She has frequent memories of tending the home and caring for the children, particularly in her mother's absence. The fact that Mrs. Balasco is able to identify with her mother implies that the rigidification of their parent-child relationship is not extreme and that movement towards the adult or parental role is tolerated. Undoubtedly the degree of behavioral reciprocity in the relationship is primarily a product of the level of parental differentiation; however, the familial roles occupied by Mrs. Balasco's older sister, Evelyn, and older brother, Jimmy, also may have served to diffuse the amount of dysfunction which otherwise would have been absorbed in Mrs. Balasco's relationship with her mother. The physical limitations of Evelyn and Jimmy facilitate their compliance with parental discouragement of growth and, thus, in comparison to their healthier siblings, Evelyn and Jimmy, remain less differentiated and more rigidly bound to their positions as children. Although both Evelyn and Jimmy occupy "loss" positions in the family, their respective disabilities limit the extent to which they can avoid amplification of the behaviors associated with the role. Thus, Mrs. Balasco's parents are not primarily invested in Evelyn or Jimmy as partners in the process of "mastering loss."

Mrs. Balasco's transition from childhood to adulthood occurs prematurely during a period of overt systemic dysfunction. When Mrs. Balasco is 12, her mother dies suddenly and family functioning is acutely disrupted as the process of "mastering loss" is temporarily rendered ineffective. Without question, this death constitutes the single most traumatic and anxiety-arousing experience in the life of the family. Both the marital and parent-child relationships are disrupted, and a substantial threat to survival is present for all remaining family members. In order to reestablish systemic stability, the process of "mastering loss" must be resumed. Resuming the process in the marital relationship requires an individual who is capable of occupying roles associated with both "loss" and "mastering" as the marriage of Mrs. Balasco's parents was based to an extent upon the mutual exchange of these positions. Reestablishing this process in relation to the children necessitates an individual who can assume the position associated with "mastering." As Mrs. Balasco becomes her mother's replacement, she occupies both the "loss" and "mastering" positions simultaneously; she becomes a substitute wife and a surrogate mother, yet she remains a child. Mrs. Balasco's earlier strong identification with her mother enables her to occupy the "mastering" position; however, the untimely death of her mother forces Mrs. Balasco and her family to confront parent-child role change prematurely. As a result, the chronic level of anxiety present in the family prior to the death of Mrs. Balasco's mother heightens as the identities of individual family members are more precarious and relational roles less well defined. In this situation, further intensification of the process of "mastering loss" occurs and the system's vulnerability to dysfunction increases.

The relative instability of the system is evidenced further as Mrs. Balasco, prematurely "cut-off" from her mother, is forced to maintain supportive contact with the family at the expense of her own growth. Her emotionally isolative stance with respect to the system, and her denial of personal needs is indicative of the extent of unresolved emotional attachment to her mother. As Mrs. Balasco functions as a mother and wife, her involvement in activities normally associated with adolescence—attending school, dating, and forming peer relationships—substantially decreases. In addition, she develops a severe ulcer condition. These signs of dysfunction reflect the level of systemic anxiety as family members attempt to continue to seek identity confirmation within a precariously stable situation.

In the following years, manifestations of systemic dysfunction increase. Jimmy is sent to live with relatives when he can no longer be cared for properly with the family. Mrs. Balasco is forced to quit school to care for the remaining family members. The process of "mastering loss" intensifies and simultaneously the potential for fragmentation of the system increases. The threat of fragmentation becomes a reality when the family is evicted from their long-standing home. At this point, Mrs. Balasco requests that she be allowed to get a job in order to help the family financially and, thus, keep family members together. Her father refuses her request, demanding instead that Mrs. Balasco remain in the home and care for the remaining children. Ultimately, Mrs. Balasco moves out of the home and goes to live with a friend who is "like a second mother." Mrs. Balasco's father is unable to care for the two remaining children himself, and is forced to send his youngest daughter, Gail, to live with another family.

This chain of events suggests that a continuation of the parent-child relationship as it existed prior to this time is not possible. A change in Mrs. Balasco's relationship to her father must, and does, occur. The relational choices posed to Mrs. Balasco by her father are the two choices which face the system. If Mrs. Balasco remains at home to care for the children, she faces the threat of behavior amplification as her father undermines her strivings for personal growth through excessive role rigidification. He assumes a position of extreme power in their relationship insisting that she remain at home in the role of the powerless caretaker.

As Mrs. Balasco and her father confront the possibility of role stagnation, the system faces the threat of relationship termination, and the process of "mastering loss" completely breaks down. If Mrs. Balasco leaves the family, her relationship to her father and siblings is altered but sustained. Although the family becomes fragmented, Mrs. Balasco's ultimate decision to marry "because Gail and Kenny still needed someone" recapitulates her earlier role in the family in which she occupied both the "loss" and "mastering" positions. Here, Mrs. Balasco is attempting to sustain systemic relationships at the expense of her own growth. Mrs. Balasco continues to confirm identity in relation to her siblings, while her father, although to a lesser degree, continues to confirm identity in relation to her.

The manner in which Mrs. Balasco and her father orchestrate this separation reflects the level of differentiation which characterizes the system at that point. Although the separation occurs, the resulting fragmentation of the family and the inability of family members to sever ties belies their precarious grip on identity and their vulnerability to dysfunction. Because Mrs. Balasco is the primary target of the FPP, she emerges from the system with a level of differentiation that is lower than that of her parents. The premature role change which Mrs. Balasco is forced to undergo as a result of the death of her mother also contributes to a lack of self-differentiation. Consequently, Mrs. Balasco's need to occupy the "mastering" position in relationships is intense and, as she pursues identity confirmation, she is more likely to rigidify relational roles, thereby increasing her vulnerability to dysfunction.

Mastering Loss in the Balascos' Families of Origin: A Comparative Summary

The process of "mastering loss" plays a part in the overall systemic functioning in the families of origin of both Mr. and Mrs. Balasco. The degree of stability which characterizes family function and the effectiveness of the process of "mastering loss" in each system is determined by a number of factors. Speculatively, the parents in each family began their married life with similar levels of individual and spouse system differentiation. However, family composition, familial relationships, and the quantity and quality of anxiety-arousing circumstances in each of the families results in variable efficacy of functioning in the respective systems. Clearly, covert and overt dysfunction is more pervasive in Mrs. Balasco's family of origin. Consequently, the vulnerability of her family to loss is greater and the process of "mastering loss" is more intensified, and paradoxically less successful.

Born during periods of extreme trauma, both Mr. and Mrs. Balasco are the primary targets of the FPP. Parent-child role rigidification occurs in both families; however, level of parental differentiation is sufficiently high to allow a reasonable degree of reciprocal behavioral complementarity within these relationships. The presence in both families of more poorly differentiated siblings serves to deflect systemic dysfunction from the Balascos' relationships with their respective parents, thereby facilitating more flexible behavioral complementarity within those relationships. The degree to which the Balascos and their respective same-sex parents are able to identify with one another earlier in their family life contributes to the manner in which parent-child role transition occurs in the following years. Overt signs of systemic dysfunction during this transition are generally minimal in both families. However, the extent to which each of the Balascos assume an emotionally isolative stance in relation to their families, and the extent to which each of the Balascos places family needs before their own needs for growth reveals the underlying degree of covert dysfunction present in their respective families.

Both Mr. and Mrs. Balasco emerge from their family systems with levels of differentiation lower than that of their parents and are, thus, more vulnerable to individual and relational dysfunction in the future. However, the more precarious stability of systemic functioning in Mrs. Balasco's family of origin makes her more vulnerable to dysfunction and more likely to intensify the process of "mastering loss" under anxiety-arousing circumstances.

The Balascos: Mastering Loss in the Current Family System

As the Balascos describe their relationship during the first several years of their marriage, overt signs of systemic dysfunction are absent. Family functioning is relatively stable as the couple pursues the task of "mastering loss" within the marital relationship. Marital fusion anxiety caused by the Balascos' respective levels of differentiation is handled by emotional distance and by a certain degree of role rigidification within the relationship. The evolution of roles within the marital context is congruent with the spouses' levels of differentiation and salient relational patterns derived from their families of origin. As the more vulnerable spouse with a slightly lower level of differentiation, Mrs. Balasco assumes the dominant role in the marriage and, later on in the family, as she becomes the primary decision-maker and disciplinarian of the children. Her initial decision to buy a house and her strong desire to conceive children reflect her need for identity confirmation within a familial context. Mrs. Balasco's orientation towards a home and parent-child relationships is reminiscent of earlier family patterns in which tending the home and caring for the children were associated with the "mastering" position. As the spouse with a slightly higher level of differentiation, Mr. Balasco assumes a more adaptive role within the marriage. He is more flexible and less dependent on familial relationships for identity confirmation. His willingness to "just pay the rent" and his neutral position regarding the conception of children underscores his ability to "master loss" outside of the family context. Notably, prior to and throughout his married life, Mr. Balasco is employed by various "institutions" and works in a supervisory role overseeing workers. His orientation towards structured and regimented work situations reflects earlier familial patterns in which authoritarian overseeing was associated with the "mastering" position. As Mrs.

Balasco goes about "mastering loss" by tending the house and later on caring for the children, and Mr. Balasco works and "brings home the bacon," each spouse is able to perceive himself or herself as occupying the "mastering" position in the relationship, while perceiving the other in the position associated with "loss." The success with which the Balascos are able to confirm their identities contributes to the stability of family functioning and to the absence of covert signs of systemic dysfunction.

The Balascos' first child, Christine, is born relatively early in the life of the family. Shortly after her birth, an element of anxiety is introduced into the system as Mrs. Balasco's father and Mr. Balasco's mother die within the same week. Predictably, the Balascos' vulnerability to loss poses a threat to systemic functioning. However, circumstances mediate the extent to which dysfunction is manifested overtly. As the Balascos describe their reactions to the deaths, they make reference to their "mastering" positions within their current family system. Mrs. Balasco explains that caring for the new baby helped her cope with the loss of her father, and Mr. Balasco asserts that taking on additional work helped him to forget his mother's death. For the Balascos, the task of "mastering loss" has shifted from the past (i.e., their families of origin) to the present (i.e., their current family). The anxiety aroused by the deaths is diffused through current systemic processes and the system outwardly remains stable. As a child born during a period of moderate trauma, Christine absorbs some degree of systemic dysfunction as the parent-child relationship is rigidified to facilitate the process of "mastering loss."

For several years following these events, the family appears to exist in a relatively anxiety-free sphere. The Balascos' retrospective description of Christine as a capable, mature youngster who frequently assumed caretaking responsibilities for her brothers suggests that early parent-child role rigidification was not extreme as Christine was allowed to identify with her mother. The amount of reciprocal behavioral complementarity allowed in Christine's relationship with her parents and, in particular, her mother, underscores the effectiveness with which the system was able to "master loss." However, the circumstances which ensue as the Balascos attempt to enlarge their family marks the beginning of a period of chronic systemic anxiety that ultimately will prove disruptive and debilitating for the family.

Anxiety is introduced into the system when Mrs. Balasco miscarries two children and concurrently becomes ill. These events prove potentially disruptive to familial roles. Mrs. Balasco's ability to gain identity confirmation in conjunction with the parenting role, or "mastering" position is undermined as she suddenly appears unable to bear children. Mr. Balasco's ability to confirm identity within the marital context is threatened as his wife becomes sickly and runs the risk of amplifying behaviors associated with the "loss" position. Tension heightens between the Balascos as the potential for identity confirmation becomes more precarious. The conception of the Balascos' second child, Teddy, against doctors' advice represents the attempts of both parents to reestablish the process of "mastering loss"; Mrs. Balasco regains the "mastering" position linked with the parental role and Mr. Balasco resumes the "mastering" position associated with producing—helping things grow. As a child born during a period of increasing systemic anxiety, Teddy absorbs a certain degree of systemic dysfunction, as under the circumstances, parent-child role ridigification is unavoidable. However, the Balascos' retrospective description of Teddy as a physically strong hard worker like his father implies that the relational role rigidification was not extreme and that a relative degree of reciprocal behavioral complementarity was permitted.

Systemic anxiety reaches its highest point, when after the birth of Teddy, physicians inform Mrs. Balasco that she has a serious blood condition and that further conception of children could seriously endanger her life. This period in the life of the system is marked by a high degree of covert individual dysfunction which, in turn, results in covert dysfunction in the spouse system, and which ultimately poses a severe threat to the survival of the system as a whole. Here, the interplay between the level of spouse differentiation and the presence of chronic anxiety substantially impairs the processes of rational decision-making in the system. Their actions determined by emotional factors, neither of the Balascos are able to develop a reasonable plan of action that could avert the potential of systemic disruption. While doctors stress the importance of a hysterectomy in order to insure Mrs. Balasco's survival, Mr. and Mrs. Balasco proceed to conceive an "unplanned" third child. Careful examination of the situation clearly indicates that their action represents an intensification of the process of "mastering loss." Mrs. Balasco's dependence on the parental role for identity confirmation makes the consideration of a hysterectomy unthinkable. Mr. Balasco's associations of infertility or barrenness with loss (i.e., loss of identity) make the operation equally unacceptable to him. The occurrence of such a situation would prove threatening to his own "mastering" position of provider and producer. The need of each of the Balascos to occupy the "mastering" position in order to confirm identity and the respective reluctance of each to occupy the "loss" position creates a dysfunctional situation in which the marital relationship is threatened by termination. That is, neither spouse seems able to assume a rational decision-making stance regarding the issue of a hysterectomy and Mrs. Balasco's safety. Here, the Balascos' desperate reliance on the process of "mastering loss" paradoxically increases the potential for overt systemic dysfunction. For each of the Balascos, Mrs. Balasco's pregnancy constitutes a potential loss of identity and, simultaneously, offers the possibility of identity confirmation. The Balascos resume occupation of the "mastering" position as the new child, Davy, occupies the "loss" position. Thus, the process of birth becomes synonymous with the process of "mastering loss" in the system. Essentially, the triumph of life forces over death forces protects the system from role stagnation and relationship termination. Signs of systemic dysfunction remain covert. Because he is born during the most severe period of anxiety for the system, Davy becomes the primary target of the FPP.

In the years to follow, several factors contribute to the relational role rigidification between Mrs. Balasco and Davy already set in motion at his birth. The continuation of Mrs. Balasco's ill health perpetuates a chronic level of systemic anxiety. Davy's development of a physical disability at the age of one introduces additional anxiety. The threat of loss in the system is pervasive and the family responds with an intensification of the process of "mastering loss." As a sick child, Davy is barely able to avoid amplification of the behaviors associated with the "loss" position. His physical disability, although not permanent, places him for roughly the first nine years of his life in a powerless dependent role. Five years after Davy's birth, Mrs. Balasco is forced to have a hysterectomy (i.e., at her physician's insistence). Thus, the potential for future identity confirmation within a parental context is permanently eliminated for her. Mrs. Balasco's relationship with Davy represents her final opportunity to occupy a "mastering" position and gain identity confirmation within the context of a parent-child relationship. Consequently, the system's vulnerability to loss of identity intensifies and a substantial amount of covert dysfunction is absorbed in Davy's relationship with his mother.

Predictably, the parent-child role change which marks the period of adolescence would be difficult for members of the Balasco family to negotiate. A number of factors, including the anxiety associated with this relational shift and the level of covert dysfunction already present in the system, contribute to the problematic nature of separation for them. However, as illustrated in an earlier review of adolescent separation in the Balascos' respective families of origin, the most important factor in the orchestration of this developmental task is the quality of the parent-child relationship, or the extent to which the separating child is involved in the process of "mastering loss." The way in which the Balascos and their adolescent children approach the task of separation is clearly indicative of earlier systemic relationships.

At the age of 18, after graduating from high school, Christine leaves the family to get married. Although Davy and his parents present different versions of this leavetaking, the fact that the Balascos are able to tolerate separating from Christine indicates the quality of relative behavioral flexibility that characterizes the parent-child relationship. Although Christine serves to absorb a certain degree of systemic dysfunction, parent-child role rigidification is not extreme and reciprocal behavioral complementarity within the relationship is tolerated. Because Christine is allowed to identify with her parents and, more specifically, her mother, she is capable of gaining identity confirmation outside the context of relationships in her family of origin. In kind, the system is able to maintain identity in her absence. Christine's transition from childhood to adulthood appears relatively free from overt manifestations of individual or systemic dysfunction. However, an examination of her life choices and the nature of her continued relationship with her family of origin reveals the presence of covert dysfunction.

Christine leaves the family to get married and, in so doing, moves immediately from one relationship system to another. Relatively early in her marriage, she has a child, although both Balascos comment that the financial situation of the couple is unstable. Christine's actions suggest that she, like her mother, requires a home and a family in order to gain identity confirmation; occupation of the caretaking parental role is associated with the "mastering" position. After she is married, Christine continues to have substantial supportive contact with her family of origin. For many years, she lives close by the family. In her capacity as a registered nurse, Christine cares for her mother, giving her weekly shots for her blood condition. Although further data with which to assess the extent of Christine's emotional cut-off from her parents are unavailable, the historical information coupled with this limited knowledge of her current life circumstances suggest that her unresolved emotional attachment to her parents is substantial.

Scrutiny of the Balasco family system after Christine's departure reveals no signs of overt dysfunction. However, a closer look at the family situation implies that Christine's involvement in the process of "mastering loss" and her stabilizing effect on family functioning was significant. Christine's familial role as caretaker served to lessen overt signs of system disruption during the periods when Mrs. Balasco was hospitalized. Christine's stance helped maintain the behavioral complementarity necessary for the continuation of the process of "mastering loss." When Christine leaves, the system's vulnerability to loss and dysfunction increases as there is no longer a mother replacement in the family. Notably, Davy associates his own withdrawal into emotional isolation with Christine's departure. Speculatively, Davy's relationship with his sister was similar to his relationship with his mother. However, from the narrative it is clear that role rigidification between brother and sister was substantially less than that between mother and son. Thus, reciprocal behavioral complementarity was permitted and Davy was able to identify at times with his sister and occasionally experience a "mastering" position. Christine's leavetaking sets off a chain of systemic reactions which ultimately undermines Davy's efforts to avoid amplification of the behaviors associated with the "loss" position (which he occupies in relation to his parents). The absence of Christine as a mother replacement creates a general level of systemic anxiety. More specifically, as one of her children leaves, Mrs. Balasco's parental responsibilities are decreased, and the subsequent threat to her identity necessitates an intensification of the mastery process. Role rigidification in Mrs. Balasco's relationships with the two remaining children increases. Because Davy is the child most involved in the process of "mastering loss," he absorbs a greater amount of covert dysfunction than his brother Teddy.

As Teddy and Davy approach adolescence, overt signs of systemic dysfunction increase as parental anxiety over the anticipated role change in the parent-child relationship heightens. The system moves into a period during which family relationships must change and, as a result, the process of "mastering loss" intensifies and the rigidification of parent-child roles increases. The level of overt dysfunction which is manifest as Teddy encounters adolescence reflects the quality of his earlier relationships with his parents. The difficulty with which the separation process is orchestrated is suggestive of the extent to which Teddy and his parents rely on their respective relationships for identity confirmation. As a child who absorbed some degree of systemic dysfunction, Teddy's level of differentiation is most likely lower than that of his parents. Consequently, he would be less capable than his parents of confirming identity outside the context of familial relationships. The fact that Teddy was allowed to identify with his parents, and particularly his father, enhances Teddy's chances to separate from the family with some degree of overt success. However, as an adult, he will undoubtedly need to continue the process of "mastering loss" in relationships outside the context of his family of origin.

As the family system strives to intensify the process of "mastering loss," Davy encounters adolescence. Davy is the child who is the primary target of the FPP and who has absorbed the greatest amount of systemic dysfunction. His role in the family has been central in perpetuating the process of "mastering loss" and in maintaining the stability of systemic relationships. The success with which Davy and his parents will be able to separate has been determined by the quality of their earlier parent-child relationships. Notably, Davy's relationships with both parents, and particularly his mother, were characterized by excessive role rigidity. Reciprocal behavioral complementarity was severely constricted. Because the Balascos relied on Davy's constant occupation of the "loss" position in order to secure their own identities, they were unable to allow him to identify with them (i.e., experience occupation of the "mastering" position). As Davy approaches the developmental task of adolescence, he is ill-equipped to make the role change that will ultimately enable him to confirm identity outside the context of family relationships. His repertoire of behaviors associated with the "mastering" position is extremely limited. Correspondingly, Davy's parents are ill-equipped to confirm their identities outside of the context of the parent-child relationship. Thus, separation constitutes a threat to identity for both Davy and his parents. Paradoxically, an avoidance of separation constitutes an equal threat to the identity of these three family members. As the Balascos, threatened by the pending adolescent separation, intensify the process of "mastering loss," relational roles become more rigidified and the interplay of parent-child behaviors becomes more constricted. The system faces the possibility of behavior amplification, role stagnation, and relationship termination. Thus, as the family confronts the changes that accompany adolescence it grapples with the issue of identity and generates a literal life and death struggle.

Faced with the threat of total identity loss if he remains in the family, Davy must leave. As relational tensions build between Davy and his mother, Davy runs from the family, taking the car on a "joy ride" to a neighboring state. With no previous driving experience, Davy literally takes his life in his hands. The impulsiveness and poor judgment which characterize his actions underscore his precarious hold on "mastery" behaviors and suggest that his ability to survive or maintain an identity apart from the family is tenuous. Concurrently, Davy's absence from the system creates an almost unmanageable level of anxiety for his parents, particularly his mother as her emotional survival, or identity, is threatened without him. Here, the dynamic balance of the system is disrupted as family members fail to negotiate complementary interaction. Davy's safe return home serves to stabilize familial relationships, as complementary behavior is resumed. Notably, both Davy and the system have survived a temporary separation. However, the threat of adolescent role change is still present and the anxiety which it produces in the system motivates the Balascos to intensify further the process of "mastering loss." As roles become increasingly more rigid, Davy and his parents again face the threat of behavioral amplification, role stagnation, and relationship termination. Thus, Davy is placed once more in the position of struggling against amplification of behaviors associated with the "loss" position. At this point, Davy's oppositional moves become more desperate. Mrs. Balasco, in the course of cleaning her son's room, reads his journal, thus gaining information regarding his plans to go out with friends. She later confronts him with this information, expressing her disapproval of his choice of friends and insisting that he terminate his activities with them. Shortly after, again while cleaning Davy's room, Mrs. Balasco finds a suicide note under his mattress. This note and two others, in addition to a suicidal gesture which Davy makes during a psychiatric hospitalization, convey both the dilemma of the family system and the solution which it seeks. Davy's suicidal behavior constitutes a concrete attempt to "master loss." As Davy makes a suicidal gesture he comes dangerously close to maximally amplifying the powerless behavior associated wih the "loss" position. When Davy survives the gesture, he struggles against behavior amplification or attempts to occupy, albeit in a primitive way, the "mastering" position. This desperate process reflects the extremely limited options available to Davy as he attempts to separate from his parents. The family system experiences the dilemma and the solution in a way similar to Davy. In order to insure the confirmation of identity, the process of "mastering loss" must continue for the Balascos. If Davy remains in the family, relational roles will stagnate and the process will come to a halt. Thus, Davy must fight his way out of the system (i.e., separate) in order to insure the continuation of the process although on a qualitatively different level. Davy's suicidal behavior represents the process of "mastering loss" for both himself and his family. Here, suicidal behavior is a desperate and overtly dysfunctional method of forcing himself and his parents to confront and master the difficult role change associated with adolescence.

The Adolescent Participants: Mastering Loss in the Present Generation

Within the limits of a one-generation perspective, the analysis of the adolescent interview material revealed clear patterns of systemic functioning that were similar to those found in the Balasco family. An overview of the data suggests that the families of the adolescent participants are engaged in the process of "mastering loss." As illustrated in the analysis of the Balasco family, numerous factors such as anxiety, level of individual differentiation, and specific family structures and processes interact to determine the effectiveness of this process within the family context. The amount of covert and overt dysfunction manifested in the family system reflects the success with which family members "master loss." Compared to their siblings, the adolescents who participated in the inquiry appear to be the family members who exhibit the highest degree of outward disturbance and they are the children who are the most involved in the process of "mastering loss" in their respective families.

The following discussion presents pertinent examples from the narratives of the adolescent participants in order to highlight the role which the process of "mastering loss" plays in their families. A review of this material illustrates the dysfunctional nature of systemic relationships and illuminates the meaning of adolescent suicidal behavior within the family context. As the adolescent participants describe themselves, their relationships with other members of their families, and events in their day-to-day lives, relational patterns associated with the process of "mastering loss" emerge. The extent of parent-child role rigidification in the families of the adolescents is notable. In particular, the data suggest that the degree of fixed behavioral complementarity between the adolescent participants and their respective parents is substantially greater than that between their parents and other children in the families. Role rigidity is apparent both in the adolescents' current relationships with their parents and in their descriptions of earlier parent-child relationships. Examples from the narratives of Linda Petite and Nancy Franklin are illustrative. Linda Petite repeatedly describes herself as an incompetent, emotionally vulnerable isolate who is "different" from other members of her family. While other family members form a cohesive, involved group, Linda experiences loneliness and exclusion. In particular, Linda's description of her mother as involved, competent, and responsible provides a striking contrast to her description of herself. Linda's relationship with her mother appears to be one in which Linda almost exclusively meets the behavioral expectations associated with the "loss" position, while Mrs. Petite almost exclusively meets the behavioral expectations associated with the "mastering" position. Similar relational patterns are evidenced in Nancy Franklin's family. Throughout her narrative, Nancy speaks of the helpless, passive, and physically vulnerable stance which she assumed in her family. Notably, other family members are depicted as the inflictors of emotional and physical pain. As Nancy describes her relationships with her parents, and in particular her relationship with her father, pronounced behavioral differences emerge. Nancy recounts numerous situations in which she passively submits to beatings from her father. These examples illustrate the manner in which Nancy consistently meets behavioral expectations linked with the "loss" position, while her father meets behavioral expectations linked with the "mastering" position with corresponding intensity.

Overall parent-child relationships are so inflexible that these adolescents are unable to identify with any of the qualities that enable their respective parents to "master" the skills of living. Consequently, as their parents continue to confirm identity through occupation of the "mastering" position, the adolescent participants are ill-equipped to avoid amplification of the behaviors associated with the "loss" position. Linda Petite captures this process when she comments:

> I believe that everybody starts out good but that there are things that happen to them along the way that stop them from growing. I feel like that happened to me . . . I feel like a lot of my life was taken away from me.

General consideration of the quality of relationships in the various families suggests that the adolescent participants are the children who are the primary targets of the FPP. Significant amounts of systemic dysfunction appear to be absorbed in these parent-child relationships and, thus, the adolescent participants contribute significantly to the family process of "mastering loss."

An examination of the manner in which the adolescent participants and their parents approach the developmental task of adolescence substantiates this point and illustrates the relational instability in the respective families. As the adolescent period approaches, the anxiety associated with the necessary parent-child role change permeates these family systems. Threatened by pending adolescent separation, the parents intensify the process of "mastering loss." Parental intensification of behaviors associated with the "mastering" position demands a corresponding amount of intensification of behaviors associated with the "loss" position. Thus, these systems face the possibility of behavior amplification, role stagnation, and relationship termination. Examples from the narrative of Nancy Franklin are particularly illustrative of this process. As Nancy moves towards adulthood, role rigidification in her relationship with her father increases significantly. Nancy's recollections of adolescence consist predominantly of instances in which her father threatens and severely beats her. The extent to which Nancy is "beaten" in adolescence far surpasses the cruelty inflicted upon her during childhood. As Nancy confronts the task of separation, she must intensify her struggle against amplification of the behaviors associated with the "loss" position. However, the quality of her earlier relationships with her parents make this struggle a difficult one and undermines the separation process. When asked what it was like to become a teenager, she explains:

> I don't know . . . things between me and my parents got worse. It got harder to know what to do to get them off my back. I got mixed up with different people, with drugs and stuff and I got into trouble with a lot of things.

These adolescents are poorly equipped to confirm identity outside the context of familial relationships and at the same time face the risk of identity negation within family relationships. As a result, they move in and out of their respective families unable to stabilize the process of "mastering loss" in either situation. The adolescents handle the "emotional cut-off" associated with the developmental task of separation by emotionally isolating themselves within the family context, or by running away from the family, or by both. The "separating" behaviors of Nancy Franklin involve a frustrating and defeating cycle in which both physical and emotional distancing mechanisms are called into play. In an attempt to avoid amplification of her behavioral role, Nancy runs away from home and thus strives for separateness in space. Distance in space is not tolerated by the family and she is forced to return home where she attempts to achieve separateness through emotional withdrawal. However, her return to the family results in an intensification of the process of "mastering loss" and once more she is faced with the threat of behavior amplification. She recalls:

> Things were always worse after I ran away. Specially with my father. He came after me and beat me up . . . he'd always beat me up when I got home.

In the case of Linda Petite, emotional isolation within the family was a major distancing mechanism. She comments:

> I'm not sure what it feels like to belong in my family. When I got older, I felt even more apart from them. My brothers and sister were involved and I don't know, I just wasn't. I felt lonelier . . .

Generally, because of the low level of system differentiation and the precarious nature of the "mastering" process in their families, any attempt that the adolescent participants make at distancing or separating is relatively ineffective. The dilemma which confronts the adolescent participants is the same dilemma which confronts their respective families. In order to insure the continuation of the process of "mastering loss" which is so crucial to the existence of family members, separation between parents and child must occur. However, for these families the very process on which they depend severely limits the alternatives for attaining separateness. The suicidal behavior of the adolescent participants may be understood as a desperate attempt to insure the continuation of the "mastering" process and the survival of systemic relationships. As the adolescents make suicidal gestures, they come dangerously close to amplifying behaviors associated with the "loss" position. As they survive these attempts, they struggle, in a desperate manner, to occupy the "mastering" position. Thus, the suicidal behavior of the adolescent participants represents the process of "mastering loss" both for themselves and for their families. Each suicidal gesture, or attempt to "master" life, represents a desperate negotiation of parent-child role change for the adolescent participants and their parents. Although this process is extremely dysfunctional, it ultimately allows these adolescents and their parents to separate. Predictably, the quality of this separation is limited and the potential for dysfunction in future relationships is significant.

Adolescent Suicidal Behavior: An Indicator of Systemic Dysfunction

Adolescent suicidal behavior is an indicator of the level of dysfunction in family systems engaged in the task of "mastering loss." To the extent that these systems view loss and separation as a threat to their survival, they enact the separation process in a manner representative of their subjective experience. The adolescents discussed here make suicide attempts. Both the nature of their behavior and the outcome reflect the efficacy of the process of "mastering loss" in their family systems.

Although the relational patterns which typify these family systems provoke life-threatening behaviors, they simultaneously undermine them. The adolescent participants and their parents are engaged in relationships with one another and, although the movement within these relationships is at times constricted, it is never static. Consequently, the life and growth forces are muted, but not stifled. It is not the intention of members of these families to separate from one another through the actual relational termination inherent in death itself. An adolescent's suicidal behavior is a desperate attempt to perpetuate the relational process of "mastering loss" thereby insuring the developmental movement necessary for continued family growth and functioning.

Bibliography

Adam, K. "Childhood parental loss, suicidal ideation, and suicidal behavior," in P. Anthony & C. Koupernik (eds.), *The Child and His Family: The Impact of Disease and Death*. New York: John Wiley & Sons, 1973.

Beck, A. *Depression*. New York: Harper & Row, 1967.

Blos, P. *On Adolescence: A Psychoanalytic Interpretation*. New York: The Free Press of Glencoe, 1972.

Boszormenyi-Nagy, I., & Spark, G. *Invisible Loyalties*. Maryland: Harper & Row, 1973.

Bowen, M. "Theory and practice of psychotherapy," in P. Guerin (ed.), *Family Therapy: Theory and Practice*. New York: Gardner Press, 1976.

Chazen, R. "Attempted suicide as a response to death wishes by members of the family," in L. Miller (ed.), *Mental Health in Rapid Social Change*. Jersualem: Jerusalem Academic Press, 1972.

Durkheim, E. *Suicide*. New York: The Free Press, 1951.

Erickson, E. *Childhood and Society*. New York: W. W. Norton Co., 1950.

Freud, A. *The Ego and the Mechanisms of Defense*. New York: International Universities Press, 1946.

Freud, S. "Mourning and melancholia," in *The Standard Edition of the Complete Psychological Works*, Vol. 14, pp. 237-258. London: Hogarth Press, 1957.

Hegel, G. (1806). *The Phenomenology of the Spirit*. Translated by J. B. Baillie. London: Swann Sonnesnschien, 1910.

Humphrey, J., French, L., Niswander, G., & Casey, T. "The process of suicide; The sequence of disruptive events in the lives of suicide victims." *Diseases of the Nervous System*, 1974, *35*, 275-277.

Kantor, D., & Lehr, W. *Inside the Family*. San Francisco: Jossey-Bass, 1975.

Kobler, A., & Stotland, E. *The End of Hope*. London: The Free Press of Glencoe, 1964.

Meerloo, J. "Suicide, menticide, and psychic homicide." *AMA Archives of Neurology and Psychiatry*, 1959, *81*, 360-362.

Menninger, Karl. *Man Against Himself*. New York: Harcourt, Brace & World, 1938.

Richman, J. "Family determinants of suicide potential," in D. Anderson & L. McClean (eds.), *Identifying Suicide Potential*. New York: Behavioral Publication, 1971.

Rosenbaum, M., & Richman, J. "Suicide: The role of hostility and death wishes from family and significant others." *American Journal of Psychiatry*, 1970, *26*.

Rosenberg, P., & Latimer, R. "Suicide attempts by children." *Mental Hygiene*, 1966, *359*, 50-354.

Sabbath, J. "The role of the parents in adolescent suicidal behavior." *Acta Paedopsychiatrica*, 1971, *38*, 211-220.

Schrut, A. "Suicidal adolescents and children." *Journal of the American Medical Association*, 1964, *188*, 1103-1107.

Speck, R. "Family therapy of the suicidal patient," in H. Resnick (ed.), *Suicidal Behaviors*. Boston: Little Brown & Co., 1968.

Stengel, E., & Cook, N. *Attempted Suicide*. England: Oxford University Press, 1958.

Stierlin, H. *Separating Parents and Adolescents*. New York: Quadrangle, 1974.

Teicher, J. "Suicide and suicide attempts," in Joseph D. Noshpitz (ed.), *The Basic Handbook of Child Psychiatry*, Vol. Two, pp. 685-697. New York: Basic Books, 1979.

Teicher, J., & Jacobs, J. "Adolescents who attempt suicide: Prelimary findings." *American Journal of Psychiatry*, 1966, *122*, 1248-1257.

Tuckman, J., & Connon, H. "Attempted suicide in adolescents." *American Journal of Psychiatry*, 1962, *119*, 228-232.

Watzlawick, P., Beavin, J., & Jackson, D. *Pragmatics of Human Communication*. New York: W. W. Norton Co., 1957.

Webster's Seventh New Collegiate Dictionary. Springfield, MA: G. & C. Merriam Co., 1970.

Yusin, A., Sinoy, R., & Nihira, K. "Adolescents in crisis: Evolution of a questionnaire." *American Journal of Psychiatry*, 1972, *129*, 574-577.

Zilboorg, G. "Differential diagnostic types of suicide." *Archives of Neurology and Psychiatry*, 1936, *35*, 270-291.

Index